KNOW ABOUT HORSES

. . . I hope you have not entirely unlearned the practice of riding on horseback. I can assure you from experience that to old age the daily ride is among the most cheering of comforts. It renews the pleasurable sensation that we are still in society with the beings and the things around us and so delightful and so necessary is this daily revival to me, that I would wish to lose that and life together. . . .

Thomas Jefferson to William
Short, April 10, 1824

KNOW
ABOUT
HORSES

—

A Ready Reference Guide to Horses,
Horse People and Horse Sports

By HARRY DISSTON

Illustrated by JEAN BOWMAN

THE DEVIN-ADAIR COMPANY
New York

For M.D.B.E.
*whose understanding and encouragement
helped so much*

Library of Congress Catalog card number: 59-13561
Manufactured in the United States of America
Book designed by Louis Koster

Distributed to the trade by
Clarkson N. Potter, Inc.
by arrangement with the Devin-Adair Company

CONTENTS

PREFACE   vii
GENERAL—BREEDS   1
HISTORICAL   15
THE HORSE IN MYTH, FABLE
   AND LEGEND   19
ANATOMY   27
STABLE MANAGEMENT   33
AILMENTS, INJURIES AND
   VICES   39
SHOEING   53
TACK   59
EQUITATION   67
THINGS TO LEARN
   BY DOING   76
HORSE SHOWS   79
FOX HUNTING   93
BEAGLING AND BASSETTING   107
STEEPLECHASING   117
FLAT RACING   125
HARNESS RACING   135
POLO   143
GYMKHANA   151
COWBOYS AND THE WEST—
   GAUCHOS   163
THE UNITED STATES
   CAVALRY   179
MOUNTED POLICE   187
MOUNTED ESCORT   191
MOUNTED DRILL   193
A TEST OF HORSEMANSHIP   194
HORSE ORGANIZATIONS   197
AMERICAN LIVESTOCK
   RECORD ASSOCIATIONS   201
BIBLIOGRAPHY   203
INDEX   208

PREFACE

This reference book is designed for the non-professional rider, the casual rider, those with a curiosity about and an interest in horses—especially beginners—boys and girls, men and women. The author has endeavored to present in a medium-sized volume essential basic information concerning the principal equestrian activities in the United States and Canada, and some fundamentals concerning the anatomy, nature, care and history of the horse. This information might be used by a beginner to learn the scope of his contemplated activity and its basic terminology; by spectators of horse events and friends (and relatives and admirers) of equestrian enthusiasts to learn something of the background, terminology and meaning of what they are watching; by experienced horsemen and horsewomen who wish to acquaint themselves with other equestrian activities in which they seldom participate, or perhaps as a refresher on some aspect of their favorite pastime; by leaders of riding groups as a basis for instruction and the preparation of test questions; by Pony Club-ers to assist in preparing for their tests, especially the oral and written ones; and perhaps even by the professionals, just to see what someone else says about what they know so well!

Know About Horses is not an encyclopedia—or a dictionary. It does attempt a sufficiently broad coverage to be really useful to the average horseman without being technical, exhaustive or overly precise. For example, some horses have nineteen ribs, but most—by a large margin —have eighteen; so in this book you will find eighteen given as the number of a horse's ribs. Again, it is well known by most knowledgeable horse people that a horse's "knee" is really not a knee joint; it corresponds to a human wrist, it is the next joint below the horse's elbow and it is at the end of the horse's forearm; the joint, anatomically, is correctly the **carpal** joint or **carpus**. But nearly all horsemen refer to this joint as the "knee"—so, in this book, the horse's carpal joint is his "knee."

The coverage is purposefully broad. Basic things about the horse—history, anatomy, ailments, stable management, shoeing, characteristics —come first; then the most usual horse activities on the North American continent—horse shows, foxhunting, steeplechasing, flat and harness

vii

racing, polo, cowboys and the West; and then some reference material generally only available in obscure manuals—mounted games, a test of horsemanship and horsemastership. Although our armed forces no longer include horse cavalry, it is included for sentimental reasons. Under "General," there is an outlined plan for a 100 mile ride (over other than mountainous country), and under "Horse Shows" there is a brief planning guide for horse show managers.

It may seem strange to find beagling and bassetting in a book about horses. This subject was included because it is very closely allied with foxhunting (mounted) and because many who follow the fox hounds on a horse also follow beagles on foot. Also, because of the great similarity of the two sports, youngsters are introduced to the technique, etiquette, conventions, traditions and lore of fox hunting through first hunting with a beagle pack in quest of a hare. It seemed, that in view of the nature of this book, a chapter on beagling was essential for completeness. I am indebted to Dr. Joseph Conolly, Master of the Buckram Beagles, for preparation of the material in this chapter.

Under each major subject, the material is organized in logical order and natural association and, with an eye to easy reference and rapid reading, key words are in bold face. There is a bibliography and an abbreviated index.

Each section has been reviewed by authorities in that field. While, unhappily, I cannot guarantee there are no errors, I believe there are none. Controversial matters have generally been excluded and with regard to a few items in which there are known differences of opinion, either both views are stated or the book includes the one which the weight of experience, sound judgment, knowledge, general acceptance and objectivity indicates is preferable.

Change and progress are a certainty. To the greatest extent, therefore, information, data and records which might require bringing them up-to-date in a relatively short time have been excluded.

Jean Bowman's attractive and expressive illustrations materially enhance the usefulness as well as the appearance of *Know About Horses,* and Captain Sydney R. Smith, squire of Bouldernoll in the pleasing Old Chatham hunting country, was most helpful and patient in assisting with a really good bibliography. To the several individuals and horse associations who painstakingly read portions of the manuscript and offered helpful suggestions, I am most grateful and appreciative.

HARRY DISSTON

Hidden Hill
Shadwell, Virginia

COLOR—The unmixed colors of a horse, from darkest to lightest, are: black, brown, bay, chestnut, dun and light gray (the usual manner of referring to a white horse). There are, of course, variations of these, such as a liver chestnut, golden chestnut, dark bay, etc.

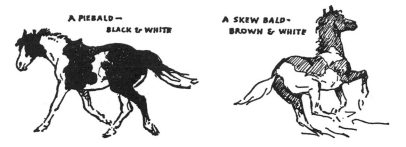

A PIEBALD—
BLACK & WHITE

A SKEW BALD—
BROWN & WHITE

A **Piebald** is a black and white horse—the white is patterned in big splotches on the black, or the reverse. Also known as **Pinto** and **Paint**.

A **Skewbald** is a bay, chestnut or brown and white patched horse—as distinguished from the **Piebald** which is black and white.

A **Roan** is a horse whose color is black, brown, bay or chestnut thickly interspersed with white. A black and white roan is usually referred to as a "blue" roan. A chestnut and white is a "strawberry" roan.

The term **Sorrel** is frequently used (but not considered correct in the best circles) to describe a light chestnut.

A **Palomino** is a horse whose hide is a golden color with a flaxen (white) mane and tail.

When the color of a horse is not immediately apparent, it is determined by the color of the hair on the muzzle and the flank.

BALD   STAR   SNIP   BLAZE   RACE OR STRIPE

MARKINGS—**Baldfaced** refers to a horse with an all white face.

A **Blaze** is a large white mark on a horse's face.

A **Race** is a narrow stripe down the center of the face.

A **Star** is a small white mark on the forehead.

A **Snip** is a small white mark near the muzzle.

3

Hogged refers to the mane clipped close to the neck.

Docked refers to the tail—the "dock," not just the hair—cut very short.

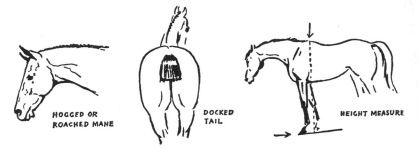

HOGGED OR ROACHED MANE   DOCKED TAIL   HEIGHT MEASURE

HEIGHT—A horse's height is measured at the withers and is expressed in terms of **hands** and **inches**. A hand is four inches. Height, then, is expressed like this: 14.3 (14 hands, 3 inches), 15.2 (15 hands, 2 inches), 16.0 (16 hands).

The height of a **pony** is, by definition, 14.2 and under.

A small horse (e.g., **polo mount**) stands from 14.3 to 15.2—the average is probably 15.1.

A **large riding horse** (e.g., a **hunter**) stands generally from 16.0 to 17.0 hands—the average probably 16.2 or 16.3.

A **heavy draft horse** stands generally from 17 to 18 hands—some Belgians reach a height of 20 hands.

WEIGHT—A horse's weight is expressed in **pounds**. In England, weight is frequently expressed as so many **stone**. A stone is 14 pounds.

A **pony** about 14 hands high would weigh from 500 to 1,000 pounds.

A **polo mount** would weigh about 900 to 1,100 pounds. The average is probably 1,000.

A **hunter** would weigh about 1,150 to 1,350 pounds. The average is probably 1,200.

A **draft horse** would weigh about 1,600 to 2,400 pounds. The average is probably 1,900.

AGE—A horse is mature at five years. An **aged** horse is one exceeding **nine** years of age.

The normal working life span of a horse is approximately **20 years**. However, many horses live well beyond that age.

The greatest age attained by a horse, according to available records which are reasonably authentic, is 53. "Clover," owned by Reverend Doctor Uriah Myers of Catawissa, Pennsylvania, is known to have been that old—or, possibly, a year or two older—when he died in 1924. "Old Bill," who died at Washington, New Jersey in 1925, is reported, but less reliably, to have been 55 at that time. It is claimed that an

English draft horse, "Billy," had reached the great age of 63 when he died in 1822.

When a horse's age is a consideration, it is assumed to be a year older January 1 of each year. Thus a foal becomes a yearling on New Year's Day following the actual date of foaling. Thoroughbreds are usually foaled in the first four months of the year.

STABLE—A **stable**—not a barn—shelters horses.

FAMILY—A **horse** or **stallion** is a natural male horse.

A **gelding** is a castrated (altered) horse. Most horses in regular use for hunting, polo, general riding, etc., are geldings. Stallions are seen, in general, only at the race track and on breeding farms.

A **mare** is a female horse.

A **foal** is a newly born horse of either sex.

A **colt** is a young male horse.

A **filly** is a young female horse. At 4 years of age she is called a mare.

A mare carries her young **eleven** months.

Horses are **foaled** or **dropped**—not "born."

A foal's father is referred to as its **sire**—a foal's mother as its **dam**. The average weight of a Thoroughbred foal—at foaling—is 120 pounds. They range from 90 to 140 pounds and, on occasion, even up to 160 pounds.

Foals are weaned from their dams at from four to six months.

A horse can get lonely. If you have only one horse (or pony), provide a companion—a dog, goat, cat, chicken. Best, you—through frequent visits, petting your horse, talking to him, giving him occasional tidbits of sugar, carrots, apples, etc., and watering, feeding and grooming him yourself—can contribute immeasurably to making him feel at home and happy. War Admiral's rabbit had to be taken from track to track. The horse sulked without his mascot.

ENDURANCE—A conditioned horse, under average favorable conditions of footing, country and weather, may be ridden about 45 miles in a day without exhaustion. This distance was actually averaged by the United States Cavalry over a three-week period foraging on the country. The Green Mountain (Vermont) Horse Association's annual contest requires riding 40 miles on each of two successive days. Greater distances, however, are not infrequent. In a Vermont endurance test, horses, largely of Morgan stock, were ridden an average of 60 miles a day for five days. On two occasions, at the U. S. Cavalry School, Fort Riley, Kansas, a squadron of Cavalry (approximately 300 horses) with full equipment and packs, was marched 100 miles in 24 hours (18 hours actual marching) and went on the next day for several miles without the loss of a horse.

5

In peacetime, a day's march for conditioned Cavalry mounts with full equipment was generally 35 miles. During a good day's hunting, one would usually cover from 20 to 40 miles.

A lightweight mount is supposed to carry up to 160 lbs., a middle-weight up to 190 lbs., a heavyweight up to 230 lbs. Cavalry mounts must carry 250 lbs.

A good draft horse can pull one-half to three-quarters of his own weight: e.g., a 2,000 pound draft horse can pull 1,000 to 1,500 pounds, one-half to three-quarters of a ton.

A Shetland pony can pull one to one-half again its own weight: e.g., a 400 to 500 pound Shetland can pull 500 to 800 pounds.

A CROSS-COUNTRY ENDURANCE RIDE—Some riding and trail associations conduct periodic endurance contests. Usually these are 100 miles to be negotiated in three days—40 miles the first day, 40 the second and 20 miles on the third day. A time limit—say 7 hours for the 40 mile phases—is established and the judging is influenced largely by the condition of the horses during and at the end of the ride. Riders cannot advance while dismounted (i.e., cannot lead their horses) and all rest periods and breaks are included in the time.

To negotiate 40 miles in 6 to 7 hours requires: 1) A planned time schedule of gaits and rests for the whole ride, and for each hour, and 2) Thorough conditioning of horse and rider—also in accordance with a plan. Included in these preparations is learning how long your horse will take to cover a mile at the walk, the trot and the canter—over a carefully measured course—on the level and over varied country, up and downhill. A good frame of reference is: **walk** one mile in 15 minutes; **trot** a mile in 7 minutes; **canter** a mile in 5 minutes. Most of the distance should be covered at a trot and a walk.

For relatively level country, the following is a plan for the 40 mile phase of a 100 mile ride. If the terrain does not permit strict adherence to the planned schedule, it is modified and adjusted so that the total minutes assigned to each gait are adhered to.

If, however, the course is over steep, mountainous country, a planned time schedule is not used; you must, of course, walk up and down the steep slopes and move along at a trot or canter on the comparatively level stretches to average out the time as best you and your horse can manage.

FORTY MILES CROSS-COUNTRY IN ONE DAY

1. *Gaits, Time and Distance*

Walk	4 mi. per hr.	1 mi. in 15 mins.	$\frac{1}{15}$ mi. in 1 min.
Trot	8½ mi. per hr.	1 mi. in 7 mins.	$\frac{1}{7}$ mi. in 1 min.
Canter	12 mi. per hr.	1 mi. in 5 mins.	$\frac{1}{5}$ mi. in 1 min.

2. *General Plan*

Complete the 40-mile ride in 6 hours, 15 minutes, including rests and a lunch break.

Proceed at an average of a little under 7 miles per hour—
4 hours at 7 miles per hour, the first hour at 6½ miles, the last at 5¾.
Rest 5 minutes at the end of the 2nd through 5th hours.
After the 3rd hour—a rest of 15 minutes (with the 5 minute rest scheduled at the end of the 3rd hour, this provides a total "break" of 20 minutes).
Start at 9:00 A.M.—Finish at 3:15 P.M.

3. *Basic Schedule*

Gait	Mins. for 1 Mile	1st	Mins. in Each Hour 2nd Through 5th	6th
Walk	15	30	20	35
Trot	7	27	30	22
Canter	5	3	5	3
Rest			5	
Total Time		60	60 (240)	60 = 6 hrs.
Miles Covered		6½	7 (28)	5¾ = 40¼

4. *Detailed Schedules for Each Hour*

First Hour Walk	Trot	Canter	Second Through Fifth Hours Walk	Trot	Canter	Rest	Sixth Hour Walk	Trot	Canter
4			3				5		
	6			7				5	
4			3				5		
	6			7				5	
4			3				5		
		1½			2½				1½
5			3				5		
	6			7				5	
4			3				5		
		1½			2½				1½
5			3				5		
	6			7				5	
4			2				5		
	3			2				2	
						5			
30	27	3 = 60	20	30	5	5 = 60	35	22	3 = 60

STRIDE—A racing horse's **stride**, from the time any hoof leaves the ground until the same hoof strikes it again, is from 20 to 26 feet.

HIGH JUMP—A horse can high jump over eight feet. Fred Wettach's **Kings Own** cleared 8 feet 3½ inches in November 1925. **Heatherbloom,** between 1901 and 1903, is reported unofficially to have cleared a height of 8 feet 3 inches. **Great Heart** jumped 8 feet and 13/16 inches on June 9, 1923 in Chicago.

BROAD JUMP—A horse can broad jump over 35 feet. Allegedly, **Chandler,** in 1847 in Warwickshire, England, jumped 39 feet. In September 1933, **Master Crump,** ridden by Larry Landsburgh, jumped 36 feet over brush and water at San Mateo, California, equalling two previous jumps of the same distance by Louis Leith's **Roustabout** and Julian Morris' **Overall** at Laurel, Maryland. The United States Army mount **Nigra** jumped 35 feet, clearing triple bars, and **Touraine,** another Army mount, jumped 33 feet.

GAITS—The natural gaits of a horse are the **walk,** the **trot** and the **gallop.** The three fastest gaits in descending order of speed are the **extended gallop,** the **pace** and the **trot.** (The **canter** is a collected gallop and generally slower than the extended trot, particularly the trot of a Standardbred racing horse.)

Acquired, or inbred gaits include the: **pace, slow gait, rack, fox trot, running walk, single foot.** (*for detailed information on gaits, see p.* 73)

NEAR AND OFF SIDE—The left side of the horse is referred to as the **near side.** The right side of the horse is referred to as the **off side.**

CROSS-COUNTRY—If you are riding cross-country and come to a stream, permit your horse to drink—even if he is hot (obviously though, not overheated or in a lather) and provided he is moved along directly after drinking. There is an ill effect only if the horse is allowed to stand after drinking.

Returning to the stable after a long or hard ride, do not remove the saddle immediately—loosen the girth and leave the saddle on the horse's back so that the blood will not return too strongly to the long compressed blood vessels under the saddle.

BREEDS

The Horse family is now represented by one genus only which includes the Horse, the Ass and the Zebra.

WILD HORSES:

The **Tarpan** or wild horse of Mongolia (also called **Przewalski's Horse**) is the only truly wild horse surviving today. About 12 hands high, it has an erect mane and lacks a forelock and is very nearly extinct.

The zebras: (A white animal with black stripes, not the reverse).

Quagga—Formerly found in South Africa; now extinct.

Burchell's Zebra. Found throughout most of southern and central Africa. There are four races.

Mountain Zebra. Southwest Africa. The smallest zebra. There are two races.

Grevy's Zebra. Ethiopia and Somaliland south into Kenya. The largest of the zebras.

Efforts to train zebras to harness or the saddle have failed.

The wild asses of Asia: A single species; three separate races.

Onager or **Persian Wild Ass.** Iran and Afghanistan.

Kulan or **Mongolian Wild Ass.** Gobi Desert.

Kiang or **Tibetan Wild Ass.** The largest of the wild asses. High plateaus of Tibet.

The wild asses of Africa: One species, two races, both very rare and approaching extinction.

Abyssinian or **Somali Wild Ass.** Somaliland, Ethiopia and Eritrea.

Nubian Wild Ass. Considered to be the ancestor of the domestic donkey. Found in the Sennar and Nubia districts of the upper Nile.

DOMESTICATED HORSES:

The **Donkey** or domesticated ass. The name derives from its supposed dun color. There are several breeds, including the **Burro**, a small donkey introduced in the Americas by the Spaniards.

The **Shetland Pony.** In its native islands 10 hands is the average height; tends to grow taller when removed from them.

The **Norwegian Dun.** Resembles the wild Tarpan; a trotter of moderate size.

The **Iceland**, or **Celtic Pony.** Resembles a coach horse in miniature; a fast trotter; with the Shetland enjoys most popularity of the eight pony breeds of the British Isles. Others include the **Welsh, New Forest, Exmoor, Dartmoor, Dales, Fell, Highland** and the Irish **Connemara.**

LIGHT HORSES:

The **Arabian Horse.** Oldest breed generally recognized, 14–15 hands. Occurs in several colors, generally bay, chestnut and gray. The **Barb** from North Africa is another desert horse related to the Arabian.

The **Hackney.** English trotting horse. Varies in size from the pony to over 16 hands. Most used in heavy and light harness. Noted for his style, smartness and high action at the trot.

EUROPEAN LIGHT BREEDS—Before the automobile, German Coach Horses **(Oldenburgers)** and French Coach Horses **(Normands)** were popular in the U. S.; a few are still used in Canada. Recently, a few stallions of the military breeds were imported from Germany—the **Trakehner** (officer's charger), the **Hannoveraner** (trooper's mount) and the **Holsteiner** (artillery) to breed to Thoroughbred and other light mares to produce weight-carrying horses of quiet disposition.

The **Cleveland Bay.** Originated in Cleveland district of Yorkshire, England. The oldest existing breed of general purpose horse suitable for riding, driving and general farm work. 16–17 hands high. Resembles a Thoroughbred and is often crossed with it.

The **Thoroughbred.** A racing breed developed in England. Three Arabian stallions laid the foundations. Bred primarily for racing. Crossed with other blood for saddle, polo, hunting and other purposes.

The **Hunter.** Not a distinct breed. Often a Thoroughbred. In Ireland the mating of Irish Thoroughbreds with Irish cart mares has produced excellent hunters.

The **Standardbred.** An American bred horse 15–16 hands high, used for trotting and pacing races. Also known as the **American Trotting Horse.**

The **American Saddle Horse.** The five gaited horse, first developed in the South by mixing Thoroughbred stock with Morgan, Canadian and the best pacers. In addition to walk, trot and canter, it demonstrates the rack and one of the three slow gaits in the ring. A horse of showy conformation, fineness and spirit.

The **Morgan Horse.** An American bred utility horse named for Justin Morgan a tavern keeper who moved from Massachusetts to Vermont taking with him a famous stallion who became the progenitor. Noted for its endurance and docility and all around ability. Average height 15½ hands.

The **Quarter Horse.** Noted for its tremendous short burst of speed especially in quarter mile races. 14¾–15 hands, muscular; stands with legs well under body; carries head low. Ideal for cattle work.

Tennessee Walking Horse. Resembles American Saddle Horse although descended from Morgan and Standardbred also. 15–16 hands high. While capable of mastering all gaits, in the show ring they exhibit three: flat-footed walk, running walk and canter. Ideal for a home stable and comfortable country riding.

The **Mustang.** Decended from horses released by Spaniards and tamed by the Indians. The name derives from the Spanish *mesteño* (wild). As **Broncos** they became the horses of wild west shows and rodeos.

DRAFT HORSES:

The **Belgian**. Heavy horse, easy disposition, roan or chestnut.

The **Shire**. A massive, heavy boned English horse, usually black.

The **Suffolk**. An English draft horse 15–16 hands, chestnut colored, lighter in weight than the Shire.

The **Clydesdale**. Scottish draft horse noted for its style. Heavier than Suffolk, lighter than Shire. Heavy hair on lower legs.

The **Percheron**. Bred originally in France, it is the most popular draft horse in America. Lighter than Shire and Belgian. Black or gray.

AMERICAN BREEDS—The distinctly American breeds are the **Standard-bred** (American trotting horse); the (gaited) **American Saddle** horse; the **Morgan** horse; the **Quarter** horse; the **Tennessee Walking** horse; and the **Mustang**.

The term **Thoroughbred** refers to a horse of extreme refinement of form and appearance, thin skin, a long slender neck, small head and ears, uniform coloring. He is extremely fast and possesses sustaining power and courage to a high degree. Horses are only properly referred to as Thoroughbreds if they are listed in the recognized Thoroughbred stud book. Thoroughbred type horses and others that are not registered, are referred to as **cold-blooded**.

The **Foundation Sires** of the **Thoroughbred** line—all imported from the East—are: The **Darley Arabian** (about 1685), the **Byerly Turk** (about 1700), and the **Godolphin Barb** (about 1725).

By curious coincidence, just a few generations later, only three direct male descendants of the three imported foundation sires remained: **Eclipse** (five generations removed from the **Darley Arabian**) foaled in 1764; **Herod**, 1758 (five generations removed from the **Byerly Turk**); and **Matchem**, 1748 (three generations removed from—grandson of—the **Godolphin Barb**). Therefore, all of today's Thoroughbreds are direct descendants also of these three.

The term *thoroughbred* is frequently used to denote *purebred* such as a "Thoroughbred Saddle Horse" or "Thoroughbred Morgan." This is incorrect usage. The correct term is *purebred* or *registered* Saddle Horse and *purebred* Morgan.

An **Orloff** is a light harness breed (trotting horse) native to and popular in Russia. From the stud of Count Orloff, it is derived of a mixture of Arabian, Dutch and Frisian blood.

Pony breeds include the **Hackney**, **Shetland**, **Welsh** and many others. However, in several breeds, in which characteristically the horse is

11

14.2 hands and over in height, animals 14.2 and under are generally classified as ponies. But, Arabian, Morgan and Palomino horses are generally classified as "horses" regardless of their height.

Chincoteague Ponies—A hardy breed of small wild pony of Moorish descent, resident on Assateague Island, Virginia—from where they are rounded up yearly on the last Thursday of July, swum across the channel to Chincoteague Island, Virginia, and sold at auction—for the benefit of the Chincoteague Volunteer Fire Department. Legend has it that they originated from survivors of a shipment of small Moorish ponies—consigned to the Viceroy of Peru to work in the gold mines of America—which were shipwrecked on Assateague Island (which shelters the Tidewater country of Virginia and Maryland) in the 16th century.

The **Lipizzan Horse**, or **Lipizzaner**, now associated almost entirely with the Spanish Riding Academy in Vienna, is distinguished by its proud and noble appearance, classic step with high knee action, daintiness of movement, lively temperament, courage, hardiness, endurance, perseverance, docility and great aptitude for training. These stylish horses were originally bred for and used to supply the royal stables with light carriage and riding horses.

The Lipizzan has a somewhat compact, well shaped body, broad chest, muscular back and strong croup, slightly pronounced withers, a thick, arched neck, a long, clean, relatively small head with expressive eyes and well set ears, and a fine mane and tail with long thick fine hair. It has short legs, strong bones and a well formed hoof. The Lipizzan varies in height between 15 and 15.3 hands. Generally it develops late and attains a greater age than other horses. Several have lived to about 33 years.

The color of Lipizzans is predominantly white; however, they are foaled dark brown and black, turning to white at about four years of age or later. There are some, but only a few, mature brown-coated Lipizzans.

The foundation stock of the Lipizzan (about 1564) was derived from Spanish horses imported to Austria from Spain and Italy (especially the **Kladruber** mixed with some Neapolitan blood). The name of the breed stems from the stud farm founded in the village of Lipizza in Austria (east of Trieste) by the Archduke Charles, son of Emperor Ferdinand I, in 1580.

The course of initial training given the Lipizzaners at the Spanish Riding Academy lasts three years and starts when they are three or four years old. Generally they reach their peak in the *haute école* (advanced dressage) at about 10 years of age. They may perform well up to 30 years of age.

12

Appaloosa—A horse which has a mottled hide—white with varying size round oblong dark spots behind the withers; black and white vertical striped hoofs and eyes showing more white than other breeds. Frequently, the horse is more solidly dark in front than behind.

Cayuse—The name applied to the Indian pony descended from the Spanish horses brought into Mexico by Cortez. It has a great deal of stamina and lives easily on the range.

The Circus Horse—There are three varieties of circus horses: (a) the white broad-backed and even-gaited draft horse used by bareback riders; (b) a horse used in high school or dressage exhibitions—fancy steps and evolutions to music—put through its paces by an attractive woman clothed in a colorful velvet. These horses are of varying size and color; (c) Liberty horses which do a variety of tricks and go through routines without a rider—wheeling, bowing, pirouetting, finding their places in line and prescribed order, etc.

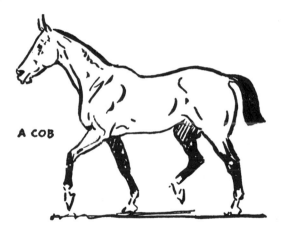

A COB

TYPES—Cob: a small stocky horse with stylish action used for driving and riding. There is a registered breed of Welsh Cobs.

A **Broomtail** is a small, slight horse not worth taming, found in rapidly decreasing numbers on the plains of the western United States.

NUMBER—Based on data obtained from the U. S. Department of Agriculture, it is estimated that there are somewhat more than two million horses in the United States. Some 400,000 of these are registered with the various breeding associations (Thoroughbreds approximately 75,000; Quarter Horses over 160,000; Standardbreds in the order of 50,000, etc.).

NEAR HORSES—The sire of a **mule** is an **ass** (jack) and its dam is a **mare**.

A **mule** is distinguished from a horse by its long ears; rat tail; smaller, narrower flinty hoof; straight back; thicker neck; proportionately bigger head; and straighter pasterns.

A **hinny** is the offspring of a stallion and a **jenny** (female ass).

A **jennet** is a small Spanish horse.

The mating of a horse and a zebra will result in an offspring called a **zebrass**.

A **charger** is an archaic military term formerly used for an officer's mount.

A **palfrey**. A light riding horse especially for ladies. Popular in the literature of knighthood.

ORIGIN—It is generally accepted that the horse descended from a small cleft-hoofed quadruped reaching its present characteristic development thousands of years ago in Asia.

APPEARANCE IN NORTH AMERICA—While fossil remains indicate that in prehistoric times horses existed in the North American continent, probably arriving by successive migrations from Asia, entire races became extinct. Horses were reintroduced to North America through Mexico by the Spaniards who brought horses with them from Europe on their voyages of exploration—the first by Cortez in 1519.

FIRST USE—Historians believe that the first use of the horse was by the Babylonians about 1700 B.C. to draw war chariots—low two-wheeled affairs of narrow trace. Others believe that primitive man learned to ride first.

The Greeks and the Assyrians used chariots extensively in battle and for racing. In 776 B.C., the Olympian Games commenced. The horse events were so popular that a separate arena was built for them called the **Hippodrome.**

FAMOUS HORSES OF FAMOUS MEN:

Alexander the Great	— *Bucephalus*
Napoleon	— *Marengo*
The Duke of Wellington	— *Copenhagen*
Robert E. Lee	— *Traveler*
George Washington	— *Nelson*
Philip Sheridan	— *Rienzi* (later changed to *Winchester*)
Zachary Taylor	— *Old Whitey*

A HORSE RUNNING AS DEPICTED IN OLD PRINTS

ACTUAL WAY HORSE RUNS

OLD PRINTS AND PAINTINGS—Horses depicted in motion prior to 1850 were characteristically incorrect. They showed a running horse

17

with an action similar to that of a dog rather than a horse. Photographs put the artists right. Drawings and paintings, prior to 1850, also tended to exaggerate the length of the neck and legs and to depict the horse's head on the small side.

The **Tang horses** of Chinese art represent the war horses of Manchu princes. They are usually depicted with open mouths and heads tossed back wildly.

ARTISTS—(illustrators, painters and sculptors) famous for their rendition of horses, include:

Prior to 20th Century

Alken, Henry T. and John
Barlow, Francis
Bonheur, Rosa
Davis, Richard Barrett
de Dreux, Alfred
Degas, H. G. E.
Ferneley, John
Géricault
Goya
Hall, Harry
Herring, John Frederick, **Sr.**
Leech, John
Marshall, Ben
Pollard, James
Troye, Edward
Sartorius, Francis and John N.
Seymour, James
Stubbs, George
Vernet, Carle
Verrocchio
Wolstenholme, **Dean**
Wootton, John

20th Century

Alden, Cecil
Anderson, C. W.
Bowman, Jean
Broadhead, Smithson
Brown, Paul
Dufy, Raoul
Edwards, Lionel
Hazeltine, Herbert
Menasco, Milton
Miner, E. H.
Munnings, Sir Alfred J.
Palmer, Lynnwood
Reeves, Richard S.
Remington, Frederic
Russell, Charles
Skeaping, John
Voss, Franklin

18

THE HORSE IN MYTH, FABLE AND LEGEND

SYMBOLS AND SUPERSTITION—The horse has been, over the ages, variously a symbol of: courage, strength, speed (swifter than eagles), the passage of time and human life, pride (get on your high horse), death (Book of Revelation, horses of The Apocalypse), and war (sacred to and sacrificed to Mars).

In the Bible, persons with military rank were generally mounted on horses—those without rank very seldom; and the association of horses with war is frequent.

A white horse signified conquest and victory and was a good omen. In medieval days (chivalry) a white horse also signified innocence and chastity.

The ancients attributed special sanctity to a vow taken on horseback —one that could not be violated.

The horse was frequently the emblem of the sun, symbolizing creative life and giving solemnity and fruitfulness to the marriage vows. The Ruler of the Day—the Sun—was drawn in his chariot by celestial horses in his daily journey across the skies. The Dawn (The Goddess Aurora) was called the "White Horse" and had Pegasus as her steed after he had disposed of his earthly rider.

To the ancient Norsemen and the Romans (Diana) the horse was also similarly associated with the moon—drawing that god's chariot across the skies.

The horseshoe in mythology represented the crescent moon. Nailed on doorways it was deemed to ward off witchcraft, the evil eye and Satan. It is still, today, a symbol of good luck. Attached to a wall or doorway, the open end should be *up*, otherwise "the luck will run out."

Horses disturbed and restless in the morning and with their manes and tails tangled and twisted are supposed, according to old English legend, to have been ridden in the night by the pixies.

SUPERSTITIONS ABOUT COLOR include these:
A good horse is never a bad color.

ONE white leg, *buy* him.
TWO white legs, *try* him.
Three white legs, *send him far away.* (Sell him to your foes)
Four white legs, *keep him not a day.* (Feed him to the crows)
(He's sure to cause you woes)
or
One white leg—buy me
Two white legs—try me
Three white legs—shy me
Four white legs—fly me

It is **lucky**—if only the **near hind** leg is white—less so (even unlucky) if it is the **off hind**!

It is **lucky** if the **forelegs**, or **hind legs**, have **equal white stockings**—**unlucky** if the foreleg and hind leg on **one side** are white—**very lucky** if the diagonal legs are white!

The Hungarians and Spanish believe all black horses are lucky—the French think the reverse.

There is an Irish superstition that a pure white horse—when ridden by the owner—confers upon him the special gift of advising how to cure physical ailments.

THE WHITE HORSE—The Saxon King Alfred in the ninth century had carved in a precipitous chalk cliff on the Berkshire Downs in England an enormous white horse, 374 feet long and 120 feet high, to commemorate his victory over the Danes at Ashdown. It is still visible today. The "Pale Horse of the Saxons," in varied forms, is found in the coat of arms of several British Regiments, of noble houses descended from the Saxons and in the ensign of Kent.

THE TROJAN HORSE—The Trojan Horse is well known to all who have read Greek history. This was the tremendous image of a mare, built of wooden planks, concealing a group of Greek soldiers. The Trojans were led to believe that this was a peace offering to the goddess Minerva by the Greeks as they ostensibly abandoned their ten year siege of Troy and sailed home. The stratagem worked. The Trojans opened their gates and widened the gap in their walls to take in the wooden mare (and its soldiers). The Greeks, under Ulysses, returned from their nearby island hideout—and Troy fell!

According to legend, Troy—built by Neptune who was the god of horses as well as the sea—was taken three times and each time a horse was the cause of its downfall. First, when the Trojan king refused a promised reward of six sacred horses to Hercules for the rescue of his daughter; second, the Greek's wooden mare (The Trojan Horse) and third, when a Greek horse stood in the gates, preventing the Trojans from shutting them against their enemies!

THE HOBBY HORSE—The Hobby Horse was originally associated with the ancient May Day festivals of English seamen—an alternative name was the "Sailor's Horse." It may have been derived from the early English "hobby," meaning a nag.

THE SAILOR'S HORSE—The terms "horse a bill" (pay for work not yet done), "pay for a dead horse" (pay for something which has been consumed or lost, or from which one will receive no return), "pull the dead horse" (work for wages that have been paid in advance) etc., stem from the old maritime custom of giving sailors a note for a month's pay in advance on signing on for a voyage. This they cashed at a sizable discount—and had fun. Thus, on sailing, they had 30 days of hard and unremunerative work ahead—"for the dead horse." Then, at the end of the payless month, they would "bury" the effigy of the "dead horse."

THE SEA HORSE—The first sea horses had a horse's head, forefeet and barrel, terminating in a fish tail—later or otherwise, the sea horse had the head of a horse and the body of a fish. Sea horses were prevalent in early Irish myths. When a tempest breaks over the sea in Ireland the breakers are said to be the white horse of the Gaelic God of the Sea.

The famous German Lorelei, after luring sailors to their destruction, left them in a sea-green chariot drawn by white horses.

The horse would, in mythological times, naturally have been associated with the wind because of his swiftness. The wind was deemed the sire of swift horses.

The horse was also associated, in ancient times, with the sea. In myth, Neptune is supposed to have created the horse in a contest with the other gods for the honor of naming what was to be the city of Athens. (However, the olive tree, created by Minerva, won out!)

NIGHTMARE—The *Nightmare* and the *"mare's nest"* do not really refer to demon horses. The terms derive from a Saxon demon vampire called Mara or Mare. This vampire rested on the chest of its sleeping victim, partially strangling him and causing fearful visions (hence nightmare). These demon vampires ("nightmares") also guarded hidden treasures, brooding over them as if they were eggs. (Hence a "mare's nest.") The harnesses of cart horses frequently were ornamented with brass charms to protect them from the witchcraft of Mare.

THE DEVIL'S HORSE—There are several English and Welsh legends in which the *Devil* appears as a *headless black horse*—and there is an American colonial legend of the Devil mounted on a black horse, defeated only by a farmer whom he was racing (or chasing), turning has grey mare into a churchyard.

THE PROPHETIC HORSES—Two immortal and prophetic horses, *Xanthus* and *Balius* drew Achilles' chariot. They were given to Achilles' father by Neptune. Xanthus prophesied Achilles' death on the battlefield.

THE CORN HORSE—Frequently a horse or mare embodied the spirit presiding over and residing in cornfields—to guard them from harm and assure the success of the crop. It was known as the "Corn Horse." The ancient Romans annually sacrificed a horse representing the corn spirit on important religious occasions.

THE UNICORN—The Unicorn is a mythological animal with the head, neck and body of a horse, the legs of a stag, the tail of a lion and with a long, twisted single horn protruding from its forehead. The Unicorn's horn was supposed to effect cures. The Unicorn is famous in heraldry as a supporter of the royal arms of Britain.

THE HIPPOGRIFF—The Hippogriff is a mythological winged animal, its forehand resembling a griffin, its barrel and hindquarters those of a horse. The Hippogriff symbolized love and transported heroes through the air.

PEGASUS—Pegasus is a mythological, white, winged horse, gifted with extraordinary speed and immortality. He carried Apollo and the Muses—and some favored and unfortunate mortal heroes—swiftly through the air. He is alleged to have sprung from the goddess Medusa when she was beheaded. Pegasus symbolizes poetic inspiration.

THE CENTAUR—The Centaur is a mythological half man, half horse—a human body, to the waist, replacing the head and neck of the horse. The Centaur symbolized the destructive and uncontrollable forces of nature and were prominent among the guardians of Hell. There were, however, some beneficial Centaurs (Chiron and Phalus)—and female Centaurs.

SAGITTARIUS—The constellation Sagittarius (The Archer) is a centaur. Mythology says that this constellation is Chiron, the "Divine Beast," placed in the sky among the stars after being put to death by Jupiter.

THE FUNERAL HORSE—Probably is a holdover from the custom of killing a dead warrior's horse and burying the horse with him. In the United States and England today it is the custom, in military funerals, to have the deceased officer's favorite charger, bridled and saddled and draped in black net and with the officer's boots reversed in the stirrups, led behind the coffin (which is on a caisson) to the grave.

In many ancient societies the favorite horses of men of noble birth —and frequently a mare and foal—were, with appropriate ceremony, slain and buried with them.

The American Comanche Indians killed, and buried with them, the horses of their dead comrades—so that they would have them to ride in the "happy hunting ground."

It was the custom of many ancient tribes to cut off the manes and tails of their horses as a symbol of mourning a departed prominent member.

There is the story of a superstitious old Irish woman who replied to a remonstrance at the killing of her dead husband's favorite horse, "D'ye think for a moment I'd let me man go on foot to the next world?"

SACRIFICE—Through the ages the horse, especially the white horse, has been considered by many peoples the most acceptable sacrifice to pagan gods—with the possible exception of human beings—for which horses (especially mares) were frequently substituted. In Plutarch's *Lives* a young mare is sacrificed in place of a virgin, to insure success in a critical battle.

The ancient Greeks, Persians, Turks, Scandinavians and Teutons practised the sacrifice of horses as the most likely to gain their gods' favors.

The ancient Greeks annually sacrificed a horse to Mars—and the ancient Persians sacrificed a white horse every month to Cyrus.

Both the Persians and American Indians sacrificed horses before committing their warriors to the crossing of a dangerous stream, so that the river's spirit might be friendly.

PATRON SAINT—The Patron Saint of horsemen is *St. George;* also associated with horses, however, were St. Stephen and St. Anthony.

THE PATRON DEITIES—The mythological gods associated with horses include: Neptune, Minerva, Hippona and Mars.

THE SUICIDE HORSE—There is a legend of recent vintage alleging that a horse named "Major"—in upstate New York—twice tried to commit suicide. First, he tried to jump off a railroad trestle 15 feet to the creek below; he caught his hind leg in the trestle and was rescued. A few days later he was found in his stall with his halter twisted around his neck and a blood vessel in his neck ruptured; he was "rescued," treated by a veterinarian and recovered.

THE SACRED NAILS—It is alleged that the Queen Mother of the Emperor Constantine the Great, prayed for and miraculously recovered the sacred nails of the Holy Cross. These, on advice of the Bishop of Jerusalem, she had made into bridle rings and attached to an especially beautiful bridle which she presented to her son, the Emperor. He decreed that the day of the revelation of the sacred nails should be honored by all as Holy Cross Day.

THE HOUYHNHNMS—The Houyhnhnms are a fabled race of horses endowed with reason, speech and noble qualities, which ruled the brutish human Yahoos—related by Swift in his *Gulliver's Travels.*

HORSE OF HIGH DEGREE—In ancient mythology it was the common practice for the gods to indicate their will to mankind through the medium of the horse—resulting in the horse being an object of considerable esteem and veneration. Perhaps, thus influenced, the Roman Emperor, Caligula, spoke of raising his horse, Incitatus, to be a consul with a view to complimenting the Gauls and Britons (then subjects of the Roman Emperor) since their people held the horse in such high regard and honor.

KING BY A NEIGH—There is a legend that, some 500 years before Christ, the Persians agreed to select as their king the contestant whose horse—mounted at a prescribed meeting place—was first to neigh. The contest and the crown were won by Darius, through a clever stratagem. He brought a mare to his horse at the specified assembly place the night before; the next day, his horse neighed almost immediately on reaching the assembly area.

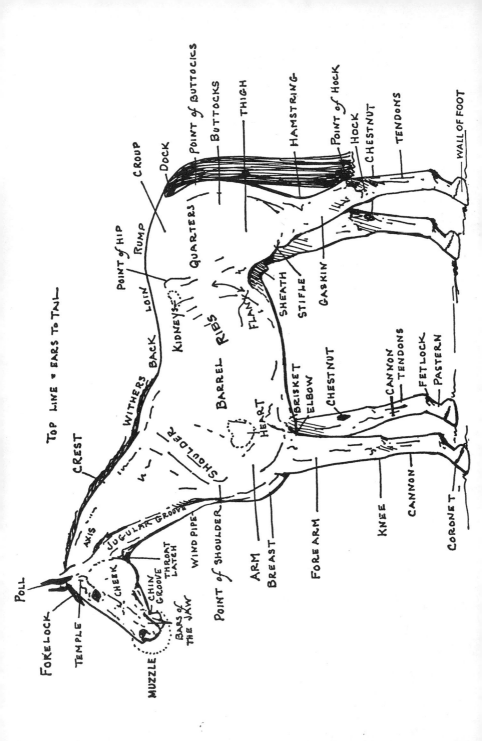

IMPORTANT POINTS OF THE HORSE:

CHESTNUTS—Chestnuts are the elongated calluses (horny structures) on the inner surface of a horse's legs. On the forelegs, they are above the knees—on the hindlegs, they are below the hocks.

RIBS—A horse has eight pairs of **true** ribs and ten pairs of **false** ribs.

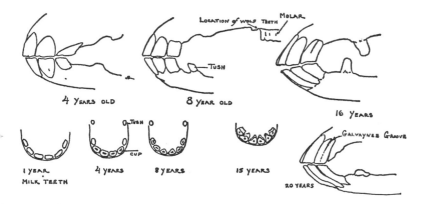

TEETH—A grown horse has 40 and sometimes 42 teeth (2 wolf teeth).
A mare has 36 and sometimes 38 (2 wolf teeth).
A foal has 24 teeth.
There are 24 molars (grinding teeth) and 12 incisors (biting teeth) and—in a male horse's mouth—4 tushes.
A horse normally has a full set of teeth at five years of age.

Tushes are pointed teeth near the front row of teeth (incisors), 2 in the lower jaw, 2 in the upper. They appear only in the male.

Wolf teeth are small rudimentary teeth which sometimes appear in front of the first molars of the upper jaw. They interfere with the action of the bit and should be removed.

Milk teeth (which precede permanent teeth) usually disappear at the age of 5.

Approximate **age** of a horse may be determined by the appearance of the teeth.

When viewed in profile, the angle between the upper and lower incisors (front teeth) becomes more acute (sloping) with age.

When viewed from the front, the teeth are somewhat separated (diverged from the middle) in a young horse and tend to converge in an old one.

When viewed toward their surface, the front teeth of a young horse are oblong in shape. As the horse grows older, the teeth become round and then triangular in appearance. The cup in the teeth of a young horse is oblong and black. As the horse grows older, the cup wears out from the center incisor teeth outward until, at 8 years, all of the lower cups are worn out. As the cups wear out they are replaced by a black line in front of the cup. In an old horse this line (the dental star) becomes round and small in the center of the tooth.

Galvayne's groove is sometimes useful in determining a horse's age. It is a well-defined vertical line (groove) close to the gums on the upper corner incisor teeth. It appears when the horse is about nine years old and extends gradually downward with advancing years.

THE STOMACH—A horse's stomach is comparatively small and there is no gall bladder. Food does not stay in it long and, when about two-thirds full, the food is forced out of it at about the rate it is consumed. It is important, therefore, to feed horses frequently and in small quantities.

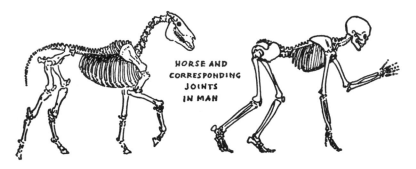

HORSE AND CORRESPONDING JOINTS IN MAN

JOINTS—The principal **joints of the foreleg** are: the shoulder, elbow, knee, fetlock, pastern, coffin (inside the hoof at the hairline). The "knee" of a horse corresponds to the wrist joint of a man—the hock to the ankle joint.

The principal **joints of the hindleg** are: the hip, stifle, hock, fetlock, pastern, coffin.

A **tendon** is an elastic fibrous cord or band attaching a muscle to a bone and transmitting the force of the muscle to the bone.

A **ligament** is an inelastic tough fibrous tissue which binds bones together to form joints.

THE HOOF—The hoof is divided into three major parts: the **wall**, the **sole** and the **frog**.

Exercise is necessary to keep a horse's feet healthy, because only by pressure and release of that pressure on the frog is blood circulated through the hoof. Thus, exercise is really the only means of nourishing the hoof and keeping it in good condition.

CONFORMATION—Conformation is a matter primarily of pleasing appearance, good structure and sound proportion for the type of horse and the type of work he is expected to do. Principal areas for determining good conformation include: the size of the head; the length and shape of the neck; the proportionate length of the back, forearms and cannons; the shape and muscle of the rump, the slope of the shoulder and pasterns; the substance of the leg or "bone"; and overall appearance.

Good shoulders for a riding horse should slope at approximately a 30 degree angle from the vertical and should have low points.

Good pasterns for a riding horse should slope at an angle from the vertical approximately 45 degrees in the forelegs and 30 degrees in the hind. If they are short and straight, the horse's gait will be choppy and uncomfortable; if they slope too much or are too long, the horse's legs will be weak.

MAJOR FAULTS OF CONFORMATION:

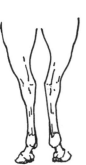  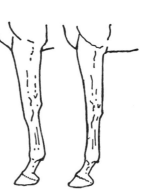

COW HOCK   SPLAY FOOT   TIED IN   CALF KNEE

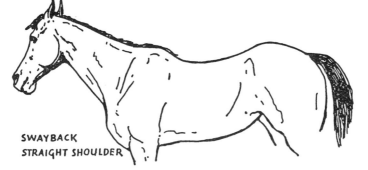

SWAYBACK
STRAIGHT SHOULDER

FAULTY GAITS—Dishing or **paddling** means swinging the forefeet sidewards when moving, especially at the trot.

31

Brushing or **interfering** refers to the interference of the inner portions of a hoof with the opposite leg so as to cause abrasions, cuts and other injuries.

Overreaching refers to the interference of a hind hoof with a foreleg, or vice versa, to cause abrasions, cuts and other injuries.

Forging is similar to overreaching except that the hind shoe strikes the fore shoe, resulting in a metallic click.

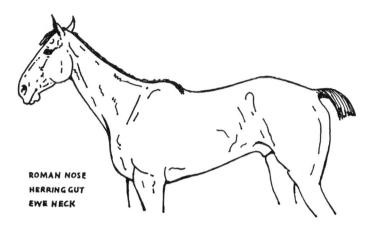

ROMAN NOSE
HERRING GUT
EWE NECK

BASIC—Regular exercise and frequent grooming (at least daily and certainly always after riding), in addition to a proper diet, are required to maintain a horse in good condition.

When approaching a horse from the rear, speak to him in a calm voice so that he will not be startled and perhaps kick.

FORAGE—The basic elements of a horse's diet are **hay** (for bulk and energy) and **oats** (for energy). However, many additional foods are needed to provide a well balanced diet. These include principally, **bran, corn** and **greens**. Other foods nutritious for horses are **barley, wheat, rice, millet, rye, beans, peas, linseed, carrots, potatoes** and **apples**. Vitamin-mineral supplements are frequently added to the regular diet.

A **bran mash** once a week is most beneficial for a horse. It is made by steeping several pounds of bran in as much boiling water as will be absorbed, stirring it well, adding a little salt and allowing it to steam until it is cool enough to eat. The mash is made either with two parts of bran to one of oats or equal parts of each.

Alfalfa, meadow hay and **clover hay** all have a high calcium-phosphorus content and are, therefore, high in bone making properties.

Corn and, to a lesser degree, **rice** and **millet** are high in fat, heat and energy-producing properties; therefore, they are most usually fed in winter.

Salt is usually fed as blocks or bricks of rock salt placed in the manger or as a "lick" in a special container on the wall near the manger.

HAY—The **hay** generally considered best for riding horses in the United States is a mixture of **upland timothy** with **clover** and some **alfalfa**.

A riding horse of medium height and weight, which is getting an average amount of work, should consume about ten pounds—from nine to twelve depending largely upon its size. Usually hay is fed before or between a feed of oats. If it is desired to reduce the amount of oats in a horse's diet and replace it with hay, a good rule of thumb would be to substitute three pounds of hay for each quart of oats.

OATS—Good oats are characterized by being plump, short, hard, of uniform size, clean, odorless, white in color; they should weigh not less than 38 pounds to a bushel; they should rattle when dropped on a solid hard surface; break sharply across when bitten and taste like good oatmeal.

A riding horse of medium height and weight, which is getting an average amount of work, should consume about ten quarts (or pounds) —from eight to twelve depending largely upon its size and the amount and severity of work—in three feeds a day. In the case of large horses and "big feeders," oats may be fed four or five times a day.

EATING AND DRINKING—Horses should be given water, hay and grain in that order. Water, given after grain, will tend to dilute its digestion; since hay provides bulk, it should be eaten before or between feeds of grain.

The tendency of some horses to bolt their food may be corrected by one of several methods: (a) including a portion, not exceeding 10%, of chaff (loose stems, leaves, flowers, etc.) with each feed; (b) spreading the feed out thinly over a large surface; (c) placing several bars over the top of the manger to divide it into compartments; or (d) placing a few large stones or other bulky non-edible substances in the manger.

When a horse is first put on grass, be careful that it does not overeat, since **flatulent colic** is almost certain to result—especially if the grass is wet or frostbitten.

BEDDING—Straw, sawdust, shavings, commercially prepared chopped sugar cane residue, and (except in damp or cold climates) peat moss and pine needles, all make good bedding for horses. Hay should *not* be used for bedding horses since horses are apt to eat it.

CONDITION—If a horse is in poor condition, but has no specific ailment, he may be brought to good condition through gradually increasing the amount of regular exercise and food progressively over a long period and grooming him thoroughly each day. Check with a veterinarian as

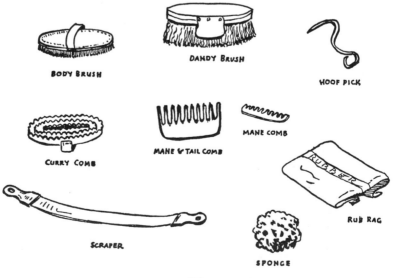

BODY BRUSH

DANDY BRUSH

HOOF PICK

CURRY COMB

MANE & TAIL COMB

MANE COMB

RUB RAG

SCRAPER

SPONGE

to a well balanced diet containing appropriate quantities of protein, minerals and vitamins.

Thrush and **canker** frequently affect a horse's hoof if the hoof is not kept clean.

GROOMING—Grooming stimulates the circulation in the horse's hide and is beneficial in improving health and appearance. Two types of brushes are usually used—a **body** brush and a **dandy** brush. These are cleaned with a curry comb. A rubber comb is used directly on the body *only* to remove caked mud and then not on the legs or head!

To determine whether a horse has been properly groomed, run the fingers through the coat against the natural lay of the hair pressing firmly against the skin. If the horse has not been properly groomed, flakes of dandruff and lines of gray will appear on the horse's coat and the tips of the fingers will be covered with scurf. Places where a thorough grooming job is frequently neglected are under the crown piece of the halter, below the ears, under the belly, on the inside of the foregoes and thighs and in the bends of the knees and hocks.

USE OF THE TWITCH

A CRIBBER

TWITCH—This is a small piece of rawhide or rope passed through a hole in a stick of wood about 2½ feet long and 1½ to 2 inches in diameter. It is used to restrain a horse by twisting the thong about his upper lip. A twitch needs to be used occasionally when a horse is shod or clipped.

STABLE VICES—The most usual stable vices are: weaving, wind-sucking, cribbing (gnawing the woodwork), biting, kicking against the stall, tail rubbing, tearing blankets, halter pulling and eating dung. For correction of vices it is best to consult a veterinarian since such measures will vary with individual horses.

SORE BACK—A sore back is prevented by using a properly fitting saddle; properly placing and adjusting the saddle; sitting properly in the saddle and not shifting the weight unduly (not slouching, sitting on the cantle, standing on one stirrup); keeping the underside of the saddle clean; dismounting occasionally on long rides to lead or rest; not removing the saddle too soon after hard work; and maintenance of good condition in the horse.

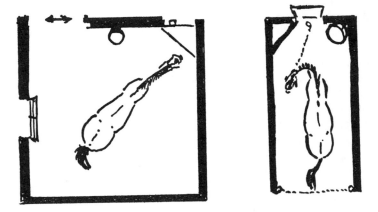

STALLS—The dimensions of a **box stall** are usually from ten to twelve feet square. A **standing** or **straight stall** is as long and half as wide.

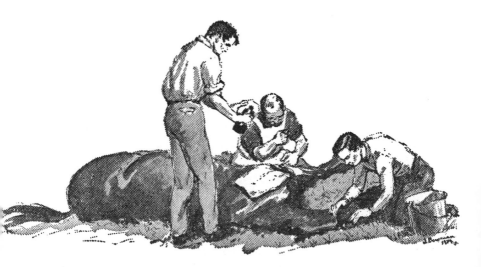

GOOD HEALTH—A horse is best maintained in good health by regular exercise suited to the horse's condition—thorough and regular grooming —a clean stable—and good shoeing. A **sound** horse is one not afflicted by defects, malfunctions, diseases, injuries or weaknesses which might affect the use to which it is being put.

INDICATIONS OF SICKNESS—Probability that a horse is sick is indicated by a generally poor **appearance** or obvious evidence of **injury** or **disorder**—and also by a quantity of **uneaten forage** in the manger, a sour or listless **disposition**, dilating nostrils, starey eyes, and by abnormal **pulse** and **temperature**.

FIRST AID—Immediate Action—The most important, imperative and immediate thing to do when a horse is badly injured, lame or sick, is to **call your veterinarian**.

Know your veterinarian's **telephone number** and, in addition, have it posted in your tack room and stable.

Until the veterinarian arrives, there are a few simple things you may do, but remember, don't try to do the doctor's job.

Severe cuts and **bleeding**—Apply firm pressure with clean cloth or bandage. Tourniquets may be used but are dangerous.

Minor wounds, abrasions and **open sores**—Clean out with a warm weak antiseptic solution (metaphen or merthiolate); then an astringent (Burow's solution) or a weak tincture of iodine and, where appropriate, dust with boracic acid powder. Avoid prolonged pressure.

Exhaustion—Place a bucket of tepid water in the horse's stall; give it a little hay, but no grain; massage its legs and back; be sure the stall has ample clean bedding. When the horse is rested, feed a bran mash and bandage its legs loosely.

Colic—Carefully administer the colic medicines prescribed by your veterinarian; walk the horse until he appears to be comfortable, keep him warm, and then place the horse in the largest stall available and see that it has ample clean bedding. **DO NOT FEED**.

Lameness—Keep the horse at rest—do not work it.

PULSE AND TEMPERATURE—A horse's normal **pulse rate** (number of beats per minute) is 36 to 40. It is usually taken under the jaw in front of the large cheek muscle—on either side, but usually on the near side.

A horse's normal **temperature** averages about 100 degrees Fahrenheit. It is taken in the rectum. The internal temperature of a healthy horse differs slightly with age, sex, breeding, time of day, proximity to exercise, extremes of weather, etc.

LAMENESS—There are three general **types** of lameness:

Supporting-leg lameness, caused by disease or injury of the bones, tendons or ligaments of the leg.

Swinging lameness, caused by disease or injury of the muscles.

Mixed lameness, caused by a combination of the preceding, and by disease or injury of the joints.

Evidence of lameness may be determined by: (a) having the horse trotted slowly on a loose lead rein toward and away from you—if practicable, on an up and down grade—and, (b) by having the horse turned sharply at a walk and trot. When making these tests, the horse should be "cold" *i.e.*, brought from the stable after rest.

Lameness in the **foreleg** is indicated by a shortened stride and the horse's head bobbing up and down noticeably. The head rises when the affected foot (or leg) touches the ground and nods when the good foot or leg touches the ground; contact of the affected foot (or leg) with the ground is relatively light and of short duration and it is carried well forward and planted well in advance of the sound foot (or leg). The sound foot is then quickly planted to relieve the weight on the affected foot (or leg).

Lameness in the **hindleg** is indicated by a shortened stride and the head bobbing up and down as in lameness of the foreleg, and, in addition, by the croup rising with the affected hindleg and dropping with the planting of the sound hindleg. The head acts opposite to the action in foreleg lameness. The head now being *down* when the affected foot (or leg) strikes the ground.

Lameness in the **shoulder** may be tested by pulling the horse's foreleg forward, then backward, as far as it will go, several times. If he flinches or tries to rear, lameness in the shoulder is indicated. If he is now trotted again, he will go more lame than before. Then walk or trot the horse over a bar; it will drag the lame leg.

Lameness is more often found in the **forelegs** than in the **hindlegs** —and most frequently in the **feet.**

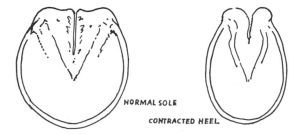

NORMAL SOLE

CONTRACTED HEEL

THE HOOF—The more common ailments include:

Bruised sole—An injury of the sensitive sole of the hoof caused by treading heavily on a sharp stone or small stump or by a badly fitted shoe.

Canker—A softening of the horn of the hoof accompanied by a moist cheese-like growth and an objectionable odor. It is caused by wet, dirty and badly drained stalls.

Contracted heels—Caused by cutting away too much of the frog of the hoof so that it does not come in contact with the ground; by cutting away of the bars which in turn causes the heels to grow inward; permitting shoes to remain on too long and lack of exercise. Contracted heels may contribute to navicular disease.

Corns—A bruise of the sensitive sole at the rear of the hoof in the angle formed by the bar and the wall, caused—as in human beings—by undue pressure of the shoe on the seat of the injury. Usually a result of improper shoeing and of shoes left on too long.

Cracked hoof or sand crack—A crack in the wall of the frog between the coronet and the shoe—usually more spread at the lower end. The hoof becomes dry, hard and brittle. It is caused by an injury to the coronary band and by rasping away the outside wall of the foot causing loss of the natural secretion which keeps the hoof moist.

Founder or laminitis—An inflammation of the sensitive laminae (hence, laminitis) directly under the horny wall of the hoof, limiting room for expansion. It is painful and usually accompanied by accelerated pulse and respiration and high temperature and, of course, heat in the affected feet. Usually affects the forefeet. There are a variety of causes: chilling from standing in a draft; drinking large amounts of water when hot; overeating of grain; eating improper or spoiled forage; prolonged work on hard surfaces; over-exertion and exhaustion.

Navicular Disease—A most serious affliction of the navicular bone in the coffin joint—almost always in the forefeet. It is caused by excessive, fast or strenuous work, especially after being turned out, and excessive work on hard roads at fast paces. Contributing causes are also contracted heels and continual use of shoes with high heels. There is some indication that a tendency to the disease may be hereditary.

Quittor—A fistulous or running sore on the coronet, usually the result of an injury to the coronet from a tread wound or overreaching, from corns or cracks and from a close nail when shoeing.

Sidebone—A bony growth on either lateral cartilage of the hoof. It is caused by fast gaits on hard roads; from a blow, wound or tread and continued use of high calks. Horses with narrow feet are more subject to the disease.

Thrush—An inflammation of the cleft of the frog—more generally affecting the hindfeet—caused by standing in a wet, dirty and badly drained stall; standing or traveling a long time in muddy water; and through infection. The disease is characterized by a foul odor; the cleft of the frog is soft and spongy and there is a thick discharge.

THE LEGS—The more common ailments include:

Arthritis—A disease affecting any of the bones from the shoulder to the hoof—found generally in older horses. The cause of the disease is not accurately known.

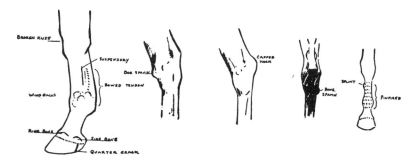

Bowed tendon—A bulge, usually in the upper portion of the rear tendon between the knee and fetlock. It is caused by a heavy strain placed upon the tendons of the front legs causing the stretching and tearing of the surrounding sheath. It is found most frequently in race horses and polo ponies.

Capped elbow or shoe boil—A noticeable swelling on the elbow, sometimes containing pus. It is usually caused through bruising by the heels or calks of the shoes of the front feet when lying down, from lack of bedding and from a rough, uneven floor.

Capped hock—A noticeable swelling on the side of the hock and sometimes a slight swelling on each side of the hock. It is caused by a horse rubbing or kicking in the stable, by a lack of bedding, by a bruise or by the kick of another horse.

Curb—A thickening and swelling of the tendons or ligaments just below the back of the hock. It is caused by undue strain from violent exertion, frequently in jumping and polo, and the resulting inflammation. Horses with "sickle hocks" and weak joints are more liable to develop curbs.

Mud fever—Broken scabby sores on the back of the pastern accompanied by a running discharge caused by too much mud and wet and from too frequent washing of the legs directly after work. The disease is similar to chapped hands in human beings.

Ringbone—A bony, ringlike enlargement high on the pastern or just above the coronet, resulting from severe work when the horse is young or from a sprain, strain or injury of the pastern. Improper care of the

44

feet may be a contributing cause. Horses with weak and excessively sloping pasterns are apt to be more susceptible to the disease as well as horses whose pasterns are too straight (because of excessive jarring).

Ruptured tendon or breaking-down—A cut or tear across the tendons (or ligaments) of the legs near the fetlock. Race horses are frequently thus affected.

Sesamoiditis—An enlargement of the bones just behind and below the fetlock joint, usually contributed to by conformation defects such as straight pasterns and feet which turn out unduly.

Splint—A bony enlargement on the side of the cannon bone where the splint bones are attached to the cannon bone in the fore or hind legs—between the knee or hock and fetlock, most frequently found in young horses. It is caused by unusual jarring of the legs when the horse is still young, e.g., jumping on hard surfaces or fast work on a hard road; by faulty shoeing causing undue pressure on the outside of the foot; and by sprains, strains and injuries in the vicinity of the splint bones.

Spavins—Bog spavin—A puffy swelling on the inside and a little to the front of the hock usually caused by a strain, by overwork, by slipping backwards and by bruises.

Bone spavin (or jack)—A bony growth inside and just below the hock joint caused by inflammation through bone friction, resulting from excessive strain such as violent effort in jumping or in galloping or trotting; slipping or sliding on hard surfaces; being suddenly pulled up on the haunches; distortion of the foot through faulty shoeing; standing on one foot too long at a time to rest an injured foot and a variety of similar causes. Younger horses are more susceptible to bone spavin.

Sprain—A tearing of a muscle, tendon or ligament due to a variety of causes: Pulling a horse up suddenly; all the weight of the body falling on one leg; excessive galloping; galloping or jumping in heavy going and on hard surfaces; excessively long toes; slipping or being cast, etc.

Stifled—Lameness produced by the kneecap (patella) on the front or inside of the stifle joint being displaced.

Strains—Undue stretching of muscles, ligaments and tendons due to the same actions which cause sprains.

Stringhalt—A distinctive, nervous, sudden snatching up of one or both hind legs when walking or trotting, and when the horse is led out of the stable or backed. Especially noticeable when the horse is "cold." The cause is not accurately known.

Swollen leg or **Big leg**—A puffy condition of the lower legs which develops after standing in the stable. It is caused by excessive work by horses in poor condition.

Thoroughpin—A round, soft, puffy enlargement in the hollows on one side (or both sides) above and back of the hock. Similar to a bog spavin, it is caused by a lack of the lubricant secretion of the joint, and by the same conditions which cause a bog spavin.

Windgall or **Windpuff**—A swelling just above and on either side of the fetlock (they do not contain air). The situations and resulting causes are generally the same (in the fetlock) as for bog spavin and thoroughpin (in the hock).

THE HIDE AND MUSCLES—The more common ailments include:

Acne—A contagious, pimply, skin eruption near the withers.

Bruises—An inflamed condition of the tissues and muscles beneath the skin caused by a blow or fall.

Eczema—An inflammation of the outer layers of the skin characterized by very small pimples which may run together and cause a discharge.

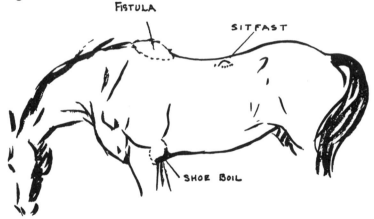

Fistules—Large pimples and abscesses on the horse's body from a variety of causes and frequently the result of an excessive amount of corn in the horse's diet.

Fistulous withers—An abscess on the withers extending toward the shoulder—caused by a blow, a poorly fitting saddle or collar, another horse's bite, or rolling on a stone.

Hide bound—Refers to skin which is inelastic to the touch, dry, dull and unattractive looking. In itself, it is not a disease, but an indication of internal disorder—frequently worms.

Itchy tail or mane—Due to a parasite or to poor condition of the blood, causing the horse to rub the tail or mane with noticeable loss of hair.

Lice—Frequently picked up from grass, giving the coat a blotchy and unattractive appearance. Horses in poor condition with insufficient grooming are susceptible to lice.

Mange—A contagious irritation of the skin which becomes thickened and wrinkled while the hair falls out, leaving small crusts. There are several types of mange, usually attacking the head, the neck, legs and root of the tail. Caused by mites, it is spread by contact.

Poll evil—An abscess on one or both sides of the poll (top of the horse's head), behind the ears; similar to fistulous withers. It is caused by hitting the head against a ceiling or beam, by halter pulling and by a tight bridle.

Ringworm—Evident through raised, circular patches of hair, usually on the neck or shoulder, which later leave grayish white crusts on the bare skin; it is caused by a fungus. The disease is highly contagious.

Sitfast—A painful swelling covered by a patch of hard, dry, scab on a horse's back—usually caused by pressure due to a poorly fitting saddle and by pressure on a sore not entirely healed.

Soreback or **Saddlesore**—Irritation caused by a poorly fitting saddle and by a saddle insecurely fixed to the horse's back because of a loose girth.

Sweeney—Shrinkage of the muscles outside the shoulder blade—usually resulting from immobilization of a foreleg for a considerable period of time, or through long continued lameness in the foreleg or foot.

Tetanus—The setting of the horse's jaw so that it can only suck nourishment—caused by a bacillus entering the blood stream through a wound.

THE STOMACH, COLON AND LUNGS—The more common ailments include:

Colic—A general term applied to a stomachache from a variety of causes: digestive disturbances, overeating, ruptured and twisted intestines, easily fermented foods such as new oats and moldy hay, parasites and indiscreet watering. There are three types: (a) **flatulent** (wind colic), (b) **spasmodic**, (c) **impaction** (constipation).

Pleurisy—An inflammation of the membranes covering the lungs, usually caused by bacterial infection.

Pneumonia—An inflammation of the lungs from the pressure of an abnormal quantity of blood in them. It frequently follows congestion of the lungs, a severe cold, influenza and strangles.

Worms—Most common of these parasites are: Bots; round, red and whip worms. Horses in poor condition are most susceptible to the development of worms. They are picked up when the horse is out at grass. The veterinarian should be consulted for both preventative and curative measures.

THE HEAD AND NECK AND SYSTEMIC—The more common ailments include:

Anthrax—A fatal disease caused by a bacillus, characterized by abnormal swelling of the throat and neck, great pain and high temperature. The horse usually dies within a few hours. Transmissible to humans.

Bronchitis—An inflammation of the throat and bronchial tubes generally caused by bacteria, exposure to cold, especially when the horse is exhausted, and by chemical and mechanical irritants. Untreated, it often leads to **heaves.**

Cold—A disease similar to that affecting human beings, caused by exposure and infection. If properly taken care of, it is not serious. (See influenza.)

Coughing—Not in itself a disease, but a frequent symptom of various diseases such as laryngitis, bronchitis, influenza, a cold, etc., or an irritation of the throat. A change from grass to grain also may cause coughing. Dampening dusty feed may prevent it.

Encephalomyelitis. Also known as **horse encephalitis,** sleeping sickness, **megrims, staggers** and **blind staggers,** is a brain infection caused by a virus believed to be transmitted by mosquitoes and ticks. Characterized by fever followed by sluggishness and muscle twitching. In between torpors, horse may "stagger" and stumble blindly into obstructions. Apt to be fatal; vaccines have been developed which prevent the disease.

Glanders or **Farcy**—A very serious communicable disease of the nasal passage characterized by ulcers on the membranes lining the nostrils, a discharge from the nostrils and small abscesses, which run together, between the angles of the lower jaw. It is usually fatal. Transmissible to humans.

Infectious Anemia also known as 'swamp,' 'malarial,' 'mountain' and 'slow' **fever.** Caused by a virus. Characterized by intermittent attacks of fever, loss of weight, progressive weakness and swelling on under parts of body and legs. Diagnosis difficult. No known cure. Animals should be destroyed and cremated to prevent spread of infection.

Influenza—A severe communicable disease evidenced by exhaustion, depression, coughing, high temperature and a catarrhal discharge from the eyes and nostrils. The origin of the disease is not accurately known. The mild type will run its course in about a week. In the more severe type (pink eye) the most critical period is the fifth to the eighth day. The disease is frequently complicated by pneumonia and is frequently fatal.

Laryngitis—An inflammation of the inner lining of the throat usually accompanied by coughing, discharge from the nostrils, difficulty in breathing, and swelling. In severe cases, the horse may be choked to death.

Strangles or **Distemper**—A very contagious disease of the nose and throat accompanied by a swelling of the glands of the throat under the jaw, a thin watery discharge from the nostrils, turning thick and yellowish, general apathy and rise in temperature. It is caused by a streptococcus which most generally attacks young horses.

THE EYES—The more common ailments include:

Cataract—A clouding of the lens of the eye, varying from a very small area to the whole area of the eye, usually caused by an injury to the eye or as a sequel to other diseases of the eye.

Conjunctivitis—An inflammation of the membrane covering the eye due to a cold, presence of foreign matter in the eye or a slight injury.

Feather—A white scar on the cornea of the eye.

Moon blindness (periodic ophthalmia)—An inflammation of the whole structure of the eye. Most common cause of blindness in horses and mules. The cause is not clearly understood. The tendency may be hereditary and it may reflect a vitamin B deficiency.

Regular ophthalmia—An inflammation of, or an abscess behind, the eyeball caused by injury or infection. It may be followed by a cataract or complete loss of sight.

THE WIND—The more common ailments include:

Broken wind (heaves)—A breakdown of the air ducts of the lungs caused by overstraining—accompanied by labored breathing, weak coughing, a slight discharge from the mouth and heaving twice when the horse exhales. It is frequently caused by excessive feeding before exercise and by dusty hay; it may be associated with a chronic cough, bronchitis, asthma, pleurisy and pneumonia, or an allergy.

High blowing—A noise made by horses when they exhale—caused by a flapping of the nostrils. This is *not* an **unsoundness**.

Roaring—A deep, hollow, prolonged cough—especially noticeable when the horse is trotted and galloped—due to disease, malformation or obstruction of the air passages, or straining of the respiratory muscles. It is sometimes accompanied by a thin nasal discharge due to improper feeding, especially of dry forage, and to poor condition.

Whistling—A shrill roaring.

STABLE VICES include: **Cribbing**—The horse swallowing air by catching hold of the manger, stall door or other convenient object with his teeth. The habit may be avoided by removing as many projections in the stall as practicable and creosoting the edges of the remainder.

Halter pulling, Kicking, Resisting saddling and bridling, Resisting grooming, Striking with the forefeet, Tail rubbing.

Weaving—A rhythmic swaying back and forth while the horse is standing in the stall.

Wind sucking—The horse swallowing air with a backward jerk of the head only (instead of cribbing).

OTHER VICES include: **Bolting** (running away), **Rearing, Shying, Interfering and brushing** (See Anatomy), **Overreaching and forging** (See Anatomy), **Dishing** (see Anatomy).

For correction of vices it is best to consult a veterinarian who will first try to determine the cause.

BREEDING PROBLEMS. The heat period in mares varies widely from two to thirty days. Most mares are in heat from two to five days. The gestation period is from 310–350 days. Conception rates are highest for mares bred on the last day or two of the heat period. A stallion usually is permitted to breed 35–40 mares each breeding season. Excessive use of a stallion (more than 3–5 times per week) reduces his fertility and lowers conception rate.

Abortions. About 50 percent of abortions in mares result from bacterial and viral infections; the causes of about 40 percent are unknown. The remainder are caused by injuries. **Contagious equine abortion** is caused by bacteria.

Diseases of Foals. Normal foals are born within 20–30 minutes after labor begins. The front feet appear first. The foal's nose is between its knees and its back is toward the back of the mare. Signals of trouble are: the appearance of only one foot or more than two; failure of the nose to appear; feet turned upside down; failure of the foal to appear within 10 minutes after the water breaks; and prolonged labor. A veterinarian should be summoned immediately.

The normal foal should be up and nursing within one or two hours after birth. Bacterial and other infections in foals are common.

ANTISEPTIC and DISINFECTANT—**Antiseptic** generally refers to a solution or powder used to prevent or arrest infections in a wound or sore.

Disinfectant refers to means to kill germs, bacteria, etc., generally on physical things but not living tissue, which might be destroyed by the strength of a disinfectant.

Perhaps the distinction may most easily be remembered this way: You use an **antiseptic** solution on your horse's sore back—you **disinfect** his stable.

STABLE MEDICAL SUPPLIES—Bearing in mind that "home doctoring" is dangerous—that when your horse is sick or lame you should call your veterinarian—you still require certain basic and simple medical supplies always at hand in your stable. The following are, in general, both adequate and ample, unless your veterinarian advises otherwise.

Alcohol, rubbing
Vaseline for lubricating scabs
Pine tar or a commercially prepared hoof dressing
Antiphlogistic poultice—as prescribed by your veterinarian
Colic medicine as prescribed by your veterinarian.
Tetanus antitoxin
Burow's solution (astringent)
Boracic acid powder (dusting)
Creolin or Lysol (disinfectants)
Metaphen (tincture) ⎱ surface
Merthiolate (tincture) ⎰ antiseptics
Iodine, tincture, regular (for abrasions)
Bandages, gauze
Bandages, woven
Cotton

BLISTER—This is a counterirritant through inflammation of the skin, rubbed on the affected part to draw the blood to that area and thus speed recovery. Commercially prepared blisters may be purchased or one may be recommended or prescribed by your veterinarian. It is usually in the form of an ointment.

PINFIRING or FIRING—Refers to the application of internal heat by puncturing the skin with fine pointed needles heated red (or even white) hot in a fire or special lamp. It is used frequently in the reduction of a sprain, curb, spavin, splint, bowed tendon and ringbone.

MALLEIN INJECTION—A test for **Glanders** given by a veterinarian. Mallein is a filtered liquid made from a culture of the glander bacilli.

DESTROYING A HORSE—When a horse has been badly hurt or is afflicted with a disease or injury which the veterinarian believes cannot be

DESTROY AT X
When a horse is destroyed
by shooting

cured, the horse is usually humanely destroyed to prevent continued suffering, pain and disability. This should always be performed by a veterinarian. Usually it is accomplished by the injection of a special drug into the jugular vein. Sometimes it is accomplished by shooting in the center of the forehead, the temple or back of the ear, with a pistol—again by a veterinarian or by someone experienced in this technique, under the supervision of a veterinarian.

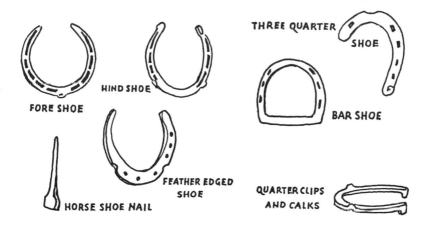

FORE SHOE

HIND SHOE

THREE QUARTER SHOE

BAR SHOE

FEATHER EDGED SHOE

HORSE SHOE NAIL

QUARTER CLIPS AND CALKS

NEED—Horses are shod to prevent the wall of the hoof wearing down to the sensitive tissue—to provide a good grip on slippery surfaces and race tracks—to protect the hoof from corns, cracks, and contracting—to induce change of gait and action—and to correct faulty hoof structure and growth.

TYPES OF SHOES—The shoes on the **fore** and **hindfeet** are different. The shoes on the forefeet are more rounded at the toe, wider and shorter than those on the hindfeet.

A **bar shoe** is one in which the usual open end is closed with a bar of metal. It is used to supply pressure or support to a particular area of the hoof such as the frog. It is used in the treatment of cracked hoofs and contracted heels and hoofs with thin soles.

A **feather edge (beveled)** is used to reduce the risk of brushing (interfering)—and to correct contraction of the heel.

A **three quarter shoe** is frequently used after the removal of corns.

NAILS—The normal shoe has seven nails—four on the outside and three on the inside. Occasionally, however, the shoes are attached with eight nails, four on each side.

CALKS—A calk is a protrusion (or sometimes a dull spike) at the toe and the heel ends of the shoe to prevent slipping. It is generally made by bending the ends down. In some instances, the calks are screwed into the shoe.

QUARTER CLIP—A quarter clip is an upward bend of the metal at the forward sides of the shoe (usually the hind) to increase the security of its attachment to the hoof and to minimize loosening from scuffing and stumbling.

PATHOLOGICAL SHOEING—Pathological shoeing refers to shoeing to

55

correct or relieve deficiencies of gait, movement, conformation, disease and lameness.

THE BLACKSMITH—or **horseshoer**, is also known as a **farrier**. The horse's shoes should generally be changed every **four** to **five** weeks. If, at the normal time for reshoeing, the shoes are very little worn, they should be removed, the hoof trimmed and the shoes reset.

The blacksmith's essential **tools** consist of: anvil, vise, hammer, tongs, knife, rasp, pincers, pritchel and buffer.

Steps in shoeing a horse are:

1. Preparation (trimming the hoof). 2. Making the shoe. 3. Fitting the shoe. 4. Driving the nails. 5. Finishing the shoe.

Correct normal shoeing is characterized by five essential features: Security of the shoe on the foot, correct nailing, maintenance of the natural level and alignment of the foot, provision for expansion of the foot, prevention of sole pressure. To put it another way, it is most important that the smith fit the shoe to the foot and not vice versa. It is important, also, that the bars of the hoof be left intact; that only the ragged edges of the frog are removed; and that the walls of the hoof are not rasped.

COLD SHOEING—This refers to nailing on a prepared shoe fitted in advance, or of a standard size, without heating or fitting it. This should be used only in an emergency, when a blacksmith is not available.

POOR SHOEING—Faulty, inexperienced or careless shoeing and unnecessary rasping result in corns, contracted heels, injuries due to improper placement of the nails and, in some cases, navicular disease. The bars of the hoof should not be removed since they are a continuation of the wall, running alongside the frog to form a buttress which keeps the heels apart. Unfortunately, the bars are frequently removed, causing sore feet.

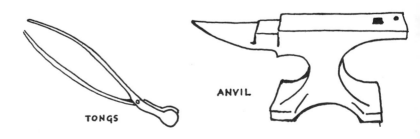

TONGS

ANVIL

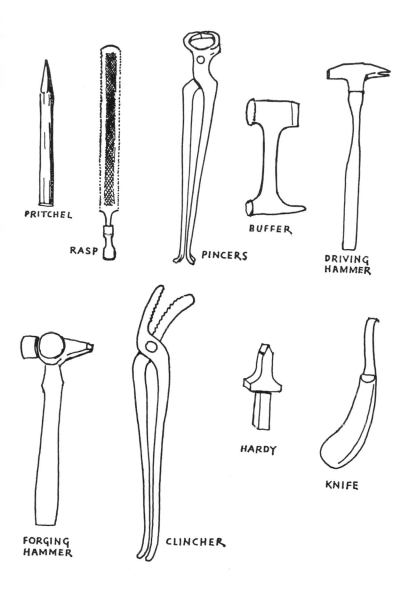

PRITCHEL

RASP

PINCERS

BUFFER

DRIVING HAMMER

FORGING HAMMER

CLINCHER

HARDY

KNIFE

BLACKSMITH'S TOOLS

57

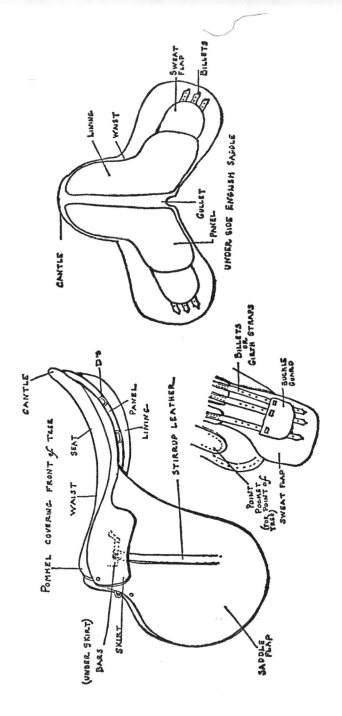

CANTLE

LINING

WAIST

SWEAT FLAP

BILLETS

GULLET

PANEL

UNDER SIDE ENGLISH SADDLE

CANTLE

D*

PANEL

LINING

SEAT

WAIST

POMMEL COVERING FRONT of TREE

STIRRUP LEATHER

(UNDER SKIRT)

BARS

SKIRT

SADDLE FLAP

BILLETS OR GIRTH STRAPS

BUCKLE GUARD

POINT POCKET (FOR POINT OF TREE)

SWEAT FLAP

COLORS—Stable colors are frequently displayed on brow bands, blankets and coolers.

ORDER OF PRECEDENCE—When tacking a horse, he should first be bridled and then saddled; when removing tack, generally the girth should be loosened and the stirrups run up on the saddle—then remove the bridle and replace it with a halter. Removing the saddle last avoids the sudden release of pressure on the horse's back.

THE SADDLE—The **pommel** is the raised forward part.

The **cantle** is the raised rear part.

The **tree** is a form over which the saddle is built. Generally, it is made of wood with metal reinforcement, but frequently, it is made of light solid metal.

The **skirts** are the small pieces of leather near the pommel covering the stirrup bars.

The **flaps** are the large pieces of leather covering the girth buckles.

The **weight** of an adult's English (flat) saddle with girth, stirrup leathers and irons, is approximately 15 to 18 pounds. Saddles vary considerably depending on their use. They are usually specially designed for the following purposes: general riding, polo, hunting, jumping, the show ring, military, flat racing, cattle work (the western or stock saddle which weighs from 30 to 40 pounds without silver).

RACING

SIDE SADDLE

OLD STYLE WESTERN

POLO *and* HUNTING

SADDLE HORSE

MILITARY

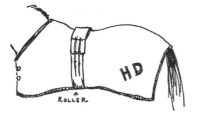

ROLLER

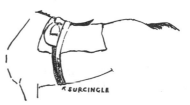

SURCINGLE

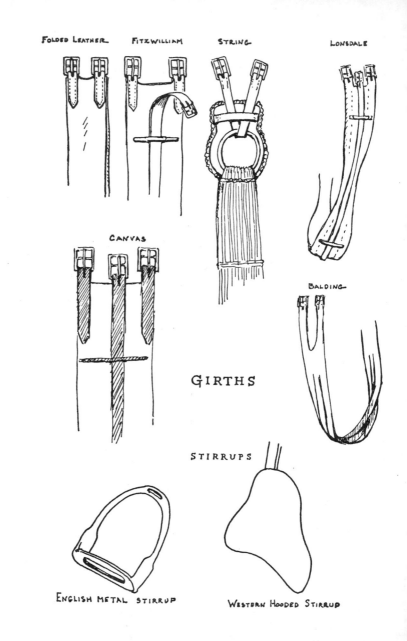

FOLDED LEATHER   FITZWILLIAM   STRING   LONSDALE

CANVAS

GIRTHS

BALDING

STIRRUPS

ENGLISH METAL STIRRUP   WESTERN HOODED STIRRUP

GIRTHS—There are several types of girth:
A **folded leather** girth is most usual.

A **balding** girth is one composed of three interlaced straps, providing freedom at the horse's elbows.

A **Fitzwilliam** girth is one with a thinner strap superimposed on the larger main girth.

A **Lonsdale** girth is shaped so that it is narrow at the horse's elbows and is reinforced with a thinner superimposed strap stitched to the main girth.

A **canvas** girth is used largely on saddle horses.

A **string** girth is used when a horse is tender or has just recovered from girth sores. It is frequently used regularly by military and police organizations.

An **overgirth** is an elastic web surcingle passing over the saddle and under the horse's belly. It is used in addition to the regular girth, generally in racing, to assure the security of the saddle.

STIRRUPS—Stirrups are generally made of metal, although, for western riding, they are generally made of wood with leather wrappings on the tread in leather hoods.

Metal stirrups are made in various sizes and weights—the widest about 5½ inches.

Metal stirrups are frequently canted toward the rear and hung off center to assist in the natural placement of the foot with heels down and toes pointing slightly upward and outward.

Stirrups on flat (English) saddles are frequently referred to as "irons."

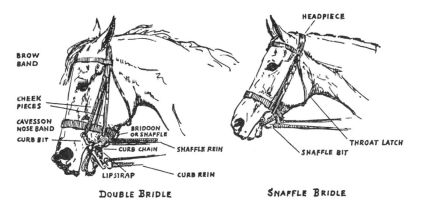

DOUBLE BRIDLE   SNAFFLE BRIDLE

BRIDLE—The bridle is usually composed of a crown piece, cheek straps, throat latch, brow band, bit, cavesson (nose band) and one or two reins.

If a curb chain is used on a bit, it is held in place along the horse's chin groove by a thin piece of leather known as a lip strap.

DROPPED NOSE BAND

HALTER AND SHANK

The bit may be attached to the bridle by a sewn-in leather loop, by buckles or by hook billets (metal fasteners in the shape of hooks).

BITS—Bits are usually made entirely of metal, but frequently the portion in the horse's mouth is made of hard rubber.

Bits are generally classified as: curb (or bit), snaffle (or bridoon), pelham or double (bit and bridoon or curb and snaffle).

A **bit** is a single bar in a horse's mouth with shanks, and a curb chain to provide leverage, controlled by a single rein.

A **snaffle** is a single bar (sometimes jointed) without a shank, controlled by a single rein.

A **pelham** is a single bar with a shank and a curb chain controlled by two reins.

A **double** bit is two separate bits—the snaffle (bridoon) and the curb (bit).

A **port** is an elliptical semicircular or inverted U-shaped hump in the middle of a bit to make it more severe and to discourage the horse putting its tongue over the bit.

A **gag** is a type of snaffle bit supported from a pulley, or through which the reins pass, so that when pressure is exerted, the bit rises in the horse's mouth.

When the bridle is placed on the horse, the following should be checked for proper adjustment:

a. the bit—regulated by the cheek straps; b. curb chain; c. throat latch; and d., if used, the cavesson (nose band).

Hackamore—A type of bridle, without a bit—used for breaking and schooling horses. Control is through pressure, just above the muzzle, instead of through pressure of a bit on the bars of the mouth.

When removing a pelham or double bridle, both the throat latch (necessarily) and curb chain should be unfastened.

When two reins are used—on a pelham or double bridle—the snaffle

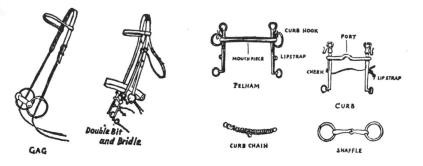

GAG

Double Bit and Bridle

PELHAM

CURB HOOK

MOUTH PIECE   LIPSTRAP

PORT

CHEEK

LIP STRAP

CURB

CURB CHAIN

SNAFFLE

reins are slightly wider (about ⅛ inch) and are fastened by a buckle. The two pieces of the curb rein are sewn together.

OTHER ITEMS—A **surcingle** is a cloth or leather band passing over a saddle or blanket to hold it fast. Sometimes also used to describe an overgirth.

A **roller** is a cloth band around the blanket at about where the middle of the saddle would rest, and padded at this point, used to hold the blanket in place.

A **cooler** is a thin, generally light wool, blanket used to cover horses while walking to "cool" them after strenuous exercise such as polo or racing.

Saddle cloths and **leg bandages** are used for special occasions and purposes.

SUPERSTITION—There is an old horsemen's superstition that the **left boot** should always be pulled on first; to do otherwise, will bring bad luck.

SADDLE SEAT

WESTERN SEAT

HUNTING SEAT

GOOD HANDS—This means that the hands are supple, sensitive, sympathetic, flexible and adaptable—maintaining a light, constant contact with the horse's mouth—thus giving a maximum control of the horse while he remains calm—with the least possible exertion on the part of the rider.

A GOOD SEAT—This means that the rider is both firm and balanced in the saddle, his legs in a position to signal and control the horse—a combination of balance, security and control. There are four basic seats (in the United States).

Hunting seat—Generally used in hunting, polo, jumping and cross-country riding, it is characterized by a position balanced over the horse's center of gravity at all gaits (and at speed, balanced on the stirrups). The back is straight, but relaxed, and head up. The thighs are in full contact with the saddle and close to the pommel, the inner portion of the legs in contact with the horse, the knee "covering" the toe, heels down, toes pointed slightly outward, elbows slightly bent and parallel to the side. "Heels down and chin up."

At gaits faster than the walk, the rider bends forward from the hips, the position of the legs remaining unchanged.

This is frequently referred to as the **Balanced**, or **Forward seat**.

Saddle horse seat—This seat is characterized by use of longer stirrups. Consequently, there is less bend in the knee and the rider appears to be sitting closer to the cantle. The stirrup irons are under the ball of the feet. The hands are generally held higher above the withers than in the forward or hunting seat, elbows are close to the side and the back is vertical.

Stock or Western seat—This seat is influenced by the heavy stock saddle with the stirrups hung further back than in the flat types of saddle. It is characterized by an almost straight leg and, as with a saddle horse, the hands are held higher above the prominent pommel.

Dressage seat—The rider is balanced vertically. Basically a hunting seat, but the rider never leaves the saddle and thus uses a longer leather for greater control.

Faults—Common faults in all seats are: Slouching in the saddle, legs too far forward ("feet on the dashboard"), stirrups too long, stirrups too short, knees not in contact with the saddle, heels level or up, reins too long and lack of control.

POOR HUNTING SEAT

STIFF WESTERN
Stirrups too long

THE AIDS—This refers to the various means by which a rider controls and communicates with the horse: his hands (the reins), his legs, weight (balance) and voice. They are used in conjunction with each other. Artificial aids include the whip, crop and spurs. The martingale, noseband, rigid reins, gag snaffle, etc. are also used to control the horse.

Direct rein refers to the use of the rein in such a way as to exert pressure to the rear in order to displace the horse's weight to the rear; this is also known as the Direct Rein of Opposition.

Indirect rein refers to the use of the rein to exert pressure to the rear toward the opposite side—in front of the withers. The horse turns to the opposite side without advancing.

Leading rein means opening out the rein away from the horse's head to move it to the right or left, by carrying the hand well out to the right or left.

Bearing rein means moving the rein against the horse's neck toward the opposite side without increased pressure to the rear. The right bearing rein is produced when the right rein acts toward the left against the right side of the horse's neck. The left bearing rein would be produced by the left rein acting toward the right against the left side of the horse's neck.

In the turn to the right on the **haunches**, the left (outside) leg is used more vigorously and further back to keep the haunches in place —along with a right leading and left bearing rein.

In the turn to the right on the **forehand**, however, the right leg is used more vigorously and further back to move the rear legs around the forelegs. The horse should remain straight from poll to croup.

70

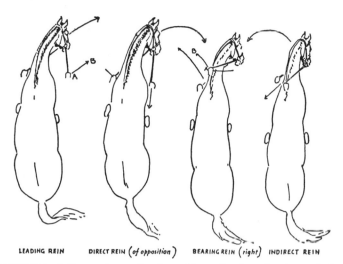

LEADING REIN   DIRECT REIN (*of opposition*)   BEARING REIN (*right*)   INDIRECT REIN

COLLECTION—A horse is perfectly collected when he is so balanced that he is able to move at any gait in any direction, forward, backward or to the side—at the slightest indication of the rider and without resistance. The degree of collection depends upon the task to be performed and the gaits desired.

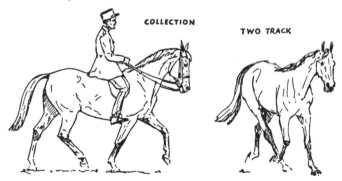

COLLECTION

TWO TRACK

TWO-TRACKING—This refers to a movement in which the horse gains ground to the front and one side simultaneously (obliquely) without turning his neck or body. Instead of moving forward on a straight line on one track, he does so on "two tracks." The horse's head is turned slightly toward the direction of movement and the shoulders slightly lead the hindquarters—the axis of the horse remaining parallel to the original line of movement.

CHANGING DIAGONALS—This refers to the rider, at the posting trot, changing his rhythm by sitting or rising an extra one-half beat so that

71

he sits (and rises) on the opposite diagonal pair of the horse's legs. Such action relieves one "diagonal" of bearing the greater part of the work and exercises the opposite "diagonal," thus, developing good balance in the horse. It also produces a helpful and healthy variety.

RIGHT LEAD

THE LEADS—The **right lead** refers to the action of a horse galloping so that he is balanced toward the right—his right forefoot being the last to leave the ground before the period of suspension. He appears to reach out or "lead" with his right forefoot. Normally, when a horse is turning or moving to the right he is on the right lead.

The **left lead** is the reverse.

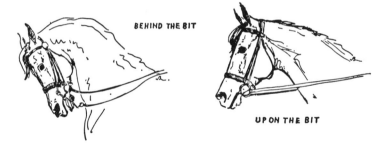

BEHIND THE BIT

UP ON THE BIT

UP ON THE BIT—This refers to contact between the bit in the horse's mouth—resting on the bars—and the rider's hands. It is achieved by urging the horse forward (he takes the bit) and feeling a light contact in the rider's hand. Thus, the horse's mouth is relaxed and alert so that he can be controlled by the action of the reins on the bit and the rider's legs.

BEHIND THE BIT—This means that the horse, by bending his neck, opening his mouth or both, deliberately slackens the reins and thereby severs communication between his mouth and the rider's hand. This situation is caused largely by reins being too long and by insufficient or improper use of the legs. Until the bit rests properly in the horse's mouth—until he takes hold of it—the rider has lost control through the use of the reins. A horse behind the bit is usually placed on the bit through vigorous use of the legs and appropriate manipulation of the reins.

THE MAJOR GAITS—The **walk**—The rhythm (number of beats in a full cycle) is FOUR. The feet strike the ground in the order—right hind, right fore, left hind, left fore. Alternately, two or three feet are on the ground at the same time. The feet are raised successively and planted in the order in which they are raised. Hoof prints of the walk would look like this:

The **trot**—The rhythm is TWO and a period of suspension. The feet strike the ground in diagonals—the right hind and the left fore almost simultaneously, the left hind and the right fore simultaneously; as the horse springs from one diagonal pair of legs to the other, all of his feet are off the ground. Hoof prints of the trot would look like this:

The **gallop**—At the slow gallop or **canter**, the rhythm is THREE and a period of suspension. The right hind; then the left hind and right fore almost simultaneously; then the left fore followed by a period of suspension when all feet are off the ground. (In this instance then, the horse would be on a left lead.) As the gallop becomes faster, a four beat gait results—because the left hind touches the ground an instant ahead of the right fore. Hoof prints of the gallop (and the canter) would look like this:

CANTER

TROT

WALK

OTHER GAITS—The **pace**—Like the trot, the rhythm is two and a period of suspension. However, the right hind and right fore strike the ground simultaneously then, following a period of suspension, the left hind and left fore simultaneously. As the horse springs from one pair of LATERAL legs to the other, all of his feet are off the ground —as in the trot.

The **rack**—A fast, four-beat gait in which the lateral legs move almost simultaneously—the hind feet striking the ground slightly before the forefeet; it is ridden faster than the trot. ("Let 'em rack.")

The **running walk**—A smooth, gliding, overstepping, four-cornered gait which is a cross between a walk and a trot. It is characteristic of the Tennessee walking horse.

73

The **fox trot**—An easy gait in which the steps are very short—a kind of jog; the horse's feet act as if he were continually changing from a walk to a trot.

The **single foot**—An easy gait in which each foot strikes the ground singly and there are alternately one and two feet on the ground; the hind feet move as in a fast walk and the fore feet as in the slow trot.

The **amble**. A slow, easy version of the pace. Sometimes used for "Single foot" in any easy gait.

The **jog** or **dogtrot**. Slower movements of the trot.

The **slow gait** or **stepping pace** is a sort of slow, collected rack, characterized by a slight swaying from side to side and animation of the forehand. Four beats.

The **lope**—A slow, easy, bounding canter on a loose rein. The term is used largely in connection with and is characteristic of the Western horse and rider.

JUMPING—When a horse lands properly after jumping, his feet normally touch the ground in this order—one forefoot then the other; then one hindfoot and the other in the same order as the forefeet (e.g., the left forefoot first, if he is on the right lead, then the right fore followed by the left hind and then the right hind).

FLEXION—This refers to relaxation (softening) of the muscles controlling the jaw and poll of the horse in yielding to the hand (and legs) of the rider. The horse's muzzle should not, however, be drawn back so that his face passes the vertical.

DRESSAGE—This is a system of training movements in which the horse's gaits are shortened and raised by bringing the balance rearward to lighten the forehand—thus giving special agility in a limited space. This is done without sacrificing extension and free movement. The result desired is that the horse will be keen but submissive and balance himself with the weight of the rider without undue strain on any set of joints or muscles. The overall objective is to enable the horse to comply easily and happily with the demands of his rider and to improve the horse's pace and bearing.

LONGEING—This refers to training or exercising a horse by causing him to move in a circle by a trainer at the end of a "longe" line (tape), long rein or rope at the various gaits. In the early stages, a whip with a long lash is used to urge the horse on, indicate speed, direction and change of gait.

A STEEP HILL—When riding down a steep hill, steady the horse's head with the reins but DO NOT hold it up unnecessarily. The horse uses his head as a balance pole. Sit perpendicular to the saddle and DO NOT slouch back.

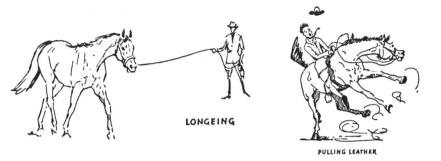

LONGEING

PULLING LEATHER

Likewise, if a horse pecks (stumbles), let him have his head so that he may see what he is doing and regain his balance. Do not "Pick him up with the reins." Again, the horse uses his head and neck as a counter balance.

SWIMMING A HORSE—Remain on the downstream side so as not to be carried against the horse by the current. (You may, however, prefer to swim your horse mounted.)

PULLING LEATHER—This should not be done. It refers to holding on to the saddle to maintain one's balance or seat, especially when a horse gets out of control or acts in a spirited manner.

SLOW TROT—At the slow trot, the rider *sits* instead of *posting* (rising to the trot).

TWO SETS OF REINS—When four reins (two sets) are used, the **snaffle** reins are held on the **outside**—the **curb** reins on the **inside**.

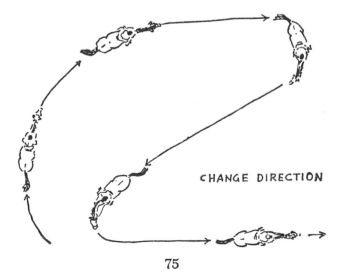

CHANGE DIRECTION

THE RIDING HALL—Those at the faster gait ride on the outside of the ring—close to the kneeboards. If someone behind you says **"track please"** give way by moving toward the center of the ring to let him pass between you and the kneeboards.

If you wish to adjust equipment, halt or dismount in the ring, first ride to the center of the ring.

Frequently, someone in authority will command **"change hands!"** At this command, (a) continue to the end of the ring, (b) turn one-half about and cross diagonally to the opposite corner, then (c) turn one-half about and continue in the opposite direction—thus the riders change from taking the track to the left to taking the track to the right or vice versa, without decreasing the gait or passing or turning in a small circle.

THINGS TO LEARN BY DOING

There are a number of things every horseman should know how to do—even if he does not have to do them often. Of course, these things could be—and no doubt are—explained in writing, but they can only be learned well and properly, and certainly more easily, by actually doing them. The following is a list of the most important:

> Bridle and saddle
> Shorten stirrup leather while
>   mounted—with one hand and
>   without removing foot from stirrup
> Tighten girth while mounted
> Run up stirrup irons
> Clean tack
> Use a leather punch

> Muck out a stall
> Bed down
> Tie a horse in a stall
> Tie a horse on a picket line
> Cross tie a horse in a stable aisle.
> Feed grain
> Feed hay
> Water
> Prepare a bran mash

> Groom a horse
> Clean a hoof

Use a currycomb
Wash a horse
Use a scraper
Clean a horse's sheath
Clean a horse's dock
Cool out a hot horse
Clip a horse

Use a twitch
Bandage a leg
Bandage a tail
Tack on a cold shoe
Braid a mane
Pull a mane
Braid a tail
Pull a tail
Take a horse's temperature
Take a horse's pulse
Use a longe line (longe a horse)
Load in a trailer
Load in a van
Help a cast horse to its feet
Catch a loose horse
Hold hand properly when feeding
tid-bits
Walk behind a horse
Open and close a gate mounted
Lead a horse over a lowered rail
Lead a horse into stall properly

Give a leg up
Accept a leg up
Vault on to a horse's back and ride
him bareback.
Pull off another's boot—with your
hand and braced against the
booted one's foot.

Light a cigarette from a lighted cigarette, mounted, walking or trotting

Tell a horse's approximate age by
its teeth

AMERICAN HORSE SHOWS ASSOCIATION (A.H.S.A.)—The governing body of horse shows is the American Horse Shows Association with headquarters in New York City. For administrative purposes, the A.H.S.A. is divided into eleven geographical zones and 19 divisions. There are 8 special committees, 11 regional committees, 21 division committees.

Officers include a Chairman of the Board, President, a First Vice President, 11 additional Vice Presidents (one representing each geographical zone), a Secretary-Treasurer, an Assistant Secretary-Treasurer, an Executive Secretary and a Recording Secretary—and there is a board of 50 Directors.

Approximately 400 shows are recognized by the American Horse Shows Association.

Horses are shown in 19 divisions. They are:

Arabian	Hunter	Roadster
Combined Training Events	Jumper	Saddle Horse
Dressage	Junior Exhibitors	Shetland Pony
Equitation	Morgan	Tennessee Walking Horse
Hackney	Palomino	Welsh Pony
Harness Pony	Parade	Western
	Polo Pony	

CLASSIFICATION OF SHOWS—Recognized shows are classified as: regular, local or honorary.

An **honor show** is one which has no violations of the A.H.S.A. rules or only a few minor ones and has been designated an Honor Show, for one year.

Shows are rated A, B and C, as a basis for reckoning points towards the Association's annual awards in the various divisions.

A—An **A** show must have a specified number of classes and premiums in the various divisions. These minimums are higher than shows with a B classification; e.g., a show with an A rating in the regular working hunter section of the Hunter Division, must have at least 6 classes and premiums totalling a minimum of $600. In the Jumper Division, there must be at least 7 classes and a minimum of $1,000 in premiums. At A shows, **triple** points toward the Division High Score Awards accrue for ribbons won.

B—Comparable figures for a **B** show are 4 classes and $300 for working hunters and 5 classes and $500 for jumpers. At B shows, **double** points toward the Division High Score Awards accrue for ribbons won.

C—A **C** show is one that does not qualify as an A or B show. At C shows, **normal** points accrue for ribbons won.

A **local** show is one which is limited by the following:
Duration not in excess of 48 hours, four sessions.
Not over sixty classes.
Cash prizes not in excess of $250 (except 100% sweepstakes).
Prize list and catalog must carry on the cover the designation "Local Show Member."
Exempt from certain regulations of the A.H.S.A.

SHOW OFFICIALS—Officers of a recognized show usually include at least a President, Vice President, Secretary and Treasurer.

The show administration also generally includes an Executive Committee, special committees, a Show Secretary and a Show Manager.

Normally the **officials** at a horse show include the **officers, judges** (one or more for each division, one or more A.H.S.A. **stewards** and **time keepers.**

Other Show Personnel include:

Ringmaster—Announcer—Recorder—Blacksmith (Shoeing smith)—"In" and "Out" Gatemen—Jump Crew—Manager and Veterinarian.

THE A.H.S.A. STEWARD—Recognized Shows are required to appoint and identify in their Prize Lists and Catalogs one or more A.H.S.A. **Stewards.**

The A.H.S.A. Steward is the representative of the American Horse Shows Association and an officer of the show. He is not to be confused with the ring steward.

A **Recognized Steward** is a person approved by the Stewards' Committee of the A.H.S.A. and issued a Steward's card. Only recognized Stewards in good standing may officiate at Recognized Shows.

The **duties** of the A.H.S.A. Steward are:

To verify the enforcement of Association rules.

To protect the interests of exhibitors.

To report to the Directors of the show any offense or violation of the rules committed by an exhibitor, judge or official.

To furnish the A.H.S.A. with a written report as to the conduct of the show within three days after its completion.

Specific application of the A.H.S.A. Steward's responsibilities include:

Verifying that all jumper courses conform to the minimum requirements.

Verifying the weighing of riders in classes requiring minimum weights.

Ascertaining that all animals in any division whose rules require it, are correctly measured.

Supervising and recording "time out" in the event of a horse casting a shoe or breaking of equipment.

Requesting that the judge ask for veterinary opinion as to the soundness of a horse, where this is considered necessary—and obtaining the veterinarian's written confirmation of any opinion rendered.

JUDGES—Recognized Judges are grouped in three classifications: **registered** (senior), **recorded** (junior) and **guest**. In all cases, they are 21 years of age or over.

Individuals who believe they are qualified apply to the American Horse Shows Association for recognition as a judge and give as references several registered judges. Based on the indicated experience, ability, judgment and character of the applicant, the Judges' Committee of the A.H.S.A. classifies the applicant as a Registered (senior) or Recorded (junior) Judge—or refuses to recognize the individual.

A **Guest Judge** is an individual member of the A.H.S.A. not enrolled as a judge, who receives special permission from the A.H.S.A. to officiate as a Registered Judge upon request of a particular show, for that show only.

There are approximately 1000 judges (Registered and Recorded) recognized by the A.H.S.A.

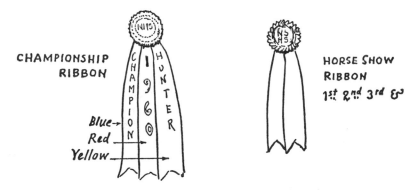

CHAMPIONSHIP
RIBBON

Blue→
Red
Yellow

HORSE SHOW
RIBBON
1ˢᵗ 2ⁿᵈ 3ʳᵈ &

RIBBONS—Ribbons are awarded to indicate the judges' placing in each class. In classes involving prize money, there are usually **four** awards —sometimes, particularly in "stakes," six. In equitation classes there are almost always **six**. In larger shows, five ribbons may be awarded in most classes and in several there may be eight awards.

In each division at least, and usually in each section, championship and reserve are awarded, based on points accumulated during the show except for horsemanship. Ribbons indicating awards are as follows:

1st Place—Blue, 2nd Place—Red, 3rd Place—Yellow, 4th Place—White, 5th Place—Pink, 6th Place—Green, 7th Place—Purple, 8th Place—Brown.

If a 9th and 10th ribbon are given, they are:
9th Place—Gray, 10th Place—Light Blue.

The colors of championship ribbons are as follows:

Grand Champion	— Blue, red, yellow and white
Reserve to Grand Champion	— Red, yellow, white and pink
Champion	— Blue, red and yellow
Reserve Champion	— Red, yellow and white

CLASSIFICATION OF INDIVIDUALS—An **amateur** is a person over 18 years of age who has not engaged in any of the professional activities listed below. Competitors in Amateur classes must have an Amateur card issued by the A.H.S.A.

A **professional** is a person who engages in horse activities either as a means of support or as a method of increasing personal income in substantial degree. Such horse activities include:

Breeding, riding, driving, schooling, training or boarding horses.
Instructing in horsemanship.
Buying, selling or dealing in horses.
Owning or managing a racing, show, schooling, livery or boarding stable for horses, or a riding academy or circus.

A professional is also one who:
Accepts employment in connection with horses in a racing, show, livery or boarding stable, riding academy or circus.
Accepts remuneration directly or indirectly for exercising, schooling, riding, driving or giving instruction.
Permits the use of his or her name, photograph or other form of personal association as a horseman or horsewoman in connection with advertisements or articles to be sold and receives a consideration for it.
One who is hired in the exclusive capacity of riding instructor, such as at a summer camp.
Any member of a professional's family (over 18) who aids or assists in the activities which make another member of the family a professional.

Children are classified as riders who have not reached their 18th birthday. For show purposes, "birthday" shall be defined as the 31st day of December following the actual date of birth.

TYPES OF CLASSES—**Maiden**—for entries which have not won **one** first ribbon (at a regular member show in the particular division in which they are shown).

Novice—for entries which have not won **three** first ribbons (at a regular member show in the particular division in which they are shown).

Limit—for entries which have not won **six** first ribbons (at a regular member show in the particular division in which they are shown).

SCORING JUMPERS—

	A.H.S.A. Rules	F.E.I. Rules
Knockdown—Front	4 faults	4 faults
Touch—Front	1 fault	No faults
Knockdown—Hind	2 faults	4 faults
Touch—Hind	½ fault	No faults
Disobedience		
(Refusal, run-out, loss of gait or forward motion, unauthorized circling)		
First	3 faults	3 faults
Second	6 faults	6 faults (cumulative)
Third	Elimination	Elimination
Fall—Horse and/or Rider	Elimination	8 faults

F.E.I.—These initials stand for **Federation Equestre Internationale**, the international body regulating horse shows with offices at Brussels, Belgium. F.E.I. rules differ from A.H.S.A. rules largely in these respects:

Time is almost always a consideration (frequently not the fastest time, but there are time limits). In most classes there is a "time allowed" and a "time limit." Exceeding the time allowed is penalized by a quarter fault for each second. Exceeding the time limit (twice the time allowed) is penalized by elimination. The time allowed is normally based on a speed of about 380 yards a minute. In some classes, it is a little less than this.

There is no distinction between a front and hind knockdown—both are penalized with four faults.

There is no penalty for touches.

A fall of horse or rider is penalized by eight faults rather than elimination.

Obstacles which jumpers have to negotiate include: the same as hunters, and in addition, triple bars, oxer, double oxer, hog back, Liverpool, parallel sheep hurdles, single bars and a variety of brightly painted obstacles.

IN AND OUT

LIVERPOOL   AIKEN   TRIPLE BAR

CROSSED POLES   HOG BACK   OXER

DOUBLE OXER   POST & RAIL (*Natural Rails*)   CHICKEN COOP

SADDLE HORSES—The gaits of a **three-gaited** saddle horse are **walk, trot** and **canter**. These horses are frequently referred to as "Walk, Trots."

The gaits of a **five-gaited** saddle horse are **walk, slow gait** (running walk, fox trot or stepping pace), **trot, rack** and **canter**.

A Combination saddle horse is one which is shown both: (a) to a four-wheeled vehicle at a walk and trot and (b) under saddle at a walk, trot and canter.

FINE HARNESS HORSE—An American Saddle Horse breed, with long mane and tail, which is shown to a four-wheeled road show wagon without top (or top down) at an animated "park gait" (trot) and at an animated walk.

Frequently the Fine Harness Horse is both driven and ridden in a "Combination Class."

REGISTERED—A **registered** horse is one whose name, identity and number are recorded in the recognized stud book of any country for its particular breed.

GREEN HORSES—Green horses are inexperienced or young horses. A green **hunter** is one that is in his first or second year of showing. A green **jumper** is one which has not shown in the jumper division at a recognized show prior to January 1st of the current year.

86

HUNTERS—In **working** hunter classes, the entry is judged entirely on performance—style of jumping, manners and way of going and even hunting pace—the extent to which they are believed to be agreeable mounts to hounds.

In **conformation** hunter classes, in addition to performance, the entry is also judged on conformation (build and appearance), quality, substance and soundness.

A **qualified** hunter is one which has been hunted regularly and satisfactorily for one or more seasons with a pack of hounds recognized or registered by the Masters of Fox Hounds Association of America or England. A letter or certificate from the Master of the pack is required.

A **corinthian** class is one in which, in addition to performance and/or conformation, consideration is given to brilliance of performance, apparel and appointments. In these classes, riders must be amateurs and members of a recognized hunt and ride in proper hunting attire.

Hunters are usually classified as:

Lightweight — Up to carrying 165 pounds
Middleweight — " " " 185 "
Heavyweight — " " " 205 "
Small — Not exceeding 15.2½ hands.
Thoroughbred — Registered in any stud book recognized by the Jockey Club

Types of **obstacles** which hunters have to jump include: natural post and rail, aiken, stone wall, chicken coop, brush, a plank fence, white gate, bank and rail, snake fence, in and out.

A SCURRY—This is a jumper class in which time is a consideration. The horse with the lowest aggregate of elapsed time in seconds, and least faults, wins.

STAKE—This is a class in which the sum of the entry fees and any added amounts is awarded to the winner and winners of the lesser awards in decreasing proportion—usually limited to horses shown in other classes in the same section or division which are not stake events. The entry fees are usually higher than in other classes.

THE HORSE SHOW CATALOG—The catalog is prepared as a result of entries made from a **prize list** which indicates the classes the show offers, with entry fees.

The catalog contains the order of events, the entries in each class, diagrams and descriptions of jumping courses, the basis on which each class will be judged, a list of exhibitors and entries (horses), the names of officers, committees and officials and other useful information. Descriptions of horses in the catalog include the horse's name, color, sex, height, age, registered number (if any) and owner.

IMPORTANT SHOWS:

East	— The National in New York
Middlewest	— The American Royal in Kansas City
Far West	— Los Angeles National Spring Show
South	— Kentucky State Fair in Louisville
Canada	— Royal Winter Fair in Toronto
England	— National Olympia in London
Ireland	— Royal Dublin Society Horse Show

OLYMPIC GAMES—In the Olympic Games, there are three equestrian events:

The **Three-Day Event** (all-around equestrian competition)—
Teams of four and individual, consisting of three phases:

1. A test of training (dressage);
2. An endurance test—consisting of a road test, cross-country and steeplechase performance;
3. A stadium jumping test.

The **Individual Dressage Competition**—
Individual, two per country.

The **Prix des Nations** (jumping competition)—
Teams of three and individual.

Each event is open to three riders and three horses from each competing nation.

TYPES OF COMPETITION under F.E.I. Rules:

Normal jumping competition—Time is not a deciding factor except in case of equality of faults.

Puissance—A test of the horse's ability to jump large obstacles.

Hunting Competition—To show obedience and handiness of the horse. There is no fixed track to follow—riders are permitted to choose the way from one obstacle to another.

Fault and out—Judging is based either on negotiating a fixed number of obstacles in the least time, or the greatest number of obstacles in a fixed time.

The six bars—Six obstacles placed in a straight line with a distance of about 12 yards between each. The obstacles are identical and may be all of the same height or at progressively increasing heights.

A.H.S.A. MEDAL CLASSES—These are open to individual junior members of the A.H.S.A. in good standing who have not reached their eighteenth birthday. There must be at least five competitors. Contestants, who qualify for any final event in any year, are eliminated from future classes during that year except in the P.H.A. (Professional Horsemen's Association of America) dressage and U.S.E.T. (United States Equestrian Team) combined tests.

JUDGES' SCORE CARD

Class No. 37

CLASS No. 37 — OPEN JUMPERS. Performance 100%. Course A.
$50, $25, $15, $10, and four ribbons.

1st	
2nd	
3rd	89
4th	104
5th	
6th	
7th	
8th	

JUMPING FAULTS

	A.H.S.A.	F.E.I.		A.H.S.A.	F.E.I.
Hind Touch	½	0	First Disobedience (Dis.)	3	3
Front Touch	1	0	Second Disobedience (Dis.)	6	6
Touch—Standard or Wing	1	0	Third Disobedience (Dis.)	Out	Out
Hind Knockdown	2	4	Refusal or Run Out	Dis.	Dis.
Front Knockdown	4	4	Showing Obstacle to Horse in Ring at		
Knockdown—Standard or Wing	4	4	Any Time	Dis.	Out
Foot in Liverpool; Water or Ditch	4	4	Loss of Forward Motion	Dis.	0
Fall of Horse or Rider	Out	8	Loss of Gait Between Start and Finish	Dis.	0
Jumping Obstacle Before It Is Reset	Out	Out	Circling, Except Upon Entering or		
Starting Before Signal or Jumping Any			After Refusal or Run Out	Dis.	Dis.
Obstacle Before the Start	Out	Out	Knockdown of Flag or Marker	Dis.	4
			Rectifying Deviation from Course	Out	Dis.
			Not Rectifying Deviation from Course	—	Out

SUGGESTED SYMBOLS FOR SCORING HUNTERS
Bold and in Stride / Satisfactory and Safe / Jumping Too Small / Popping / In Too Close / Too Far Back / Diving / Propping / Twisting Over / Weaving / Legs Down

Horse No.	JUMP NUMBERS (if More Than 10 Jumps, Mark No. 1 Lower Block, etc)										Out Over	Total Faults	HUNTER SCORING			F E I
	(1)	2	3	(4)	(5)	6	7	8					Manners and Way of Going	Hunting Pace	Style of Jumping	Bonfar marking
31	/	–	–	3½	–	–	–	/				11				9
153	–	2	–	–	–	–	–	–				2				4
107	–	–	–	–	4	–	–	–				4				4
8	½	–	3/4	–	/	2	4/–	–				16½				17
92	–	–	–	–/	3/4	4/x	—					X				X
144	–	–	–	–	–	–	–	–				0	Jump off			0
105	/	–	–	2	2	–	–	½				5½				8
77	–	–	–	–	–	3/–	–			5½		3				3
156	–	/	–	½	/	½	–	/		4		4				0
89	–	–	/	–	–	–	–			3		1	(3)			0
112	½	–	½	–	–	–	–	/		2		2				0
16	–	–	–	–	–	4 Fall	—					X	To this point {		12	
120	½	/	/									X	To that point {		0	
163	–	–	–	–	–	–	–					0	Jump off			0
104	–	/	–	–	–	–	½			2		1½	(4)			0

Judge's Score Card—Open Jumpers

The circled numbers indicate the obstacles for which this judge is primarily responsible.

∩ indicates that these two obstacles are a "combination." If a horse refuses the second element, it must then rejump both the first and second elements of the combination.

↓ indicates that the course is composed of 8 obstacles (jumps).

— indicates no faults at that obstacle ("clean").

3/- indicates a refusal; the figure or mark beneath the slash indicates the scoring when the same obstacle is jumped again after the refusal.

X indicates elimination.

Nos. 144 and 163 would attempt to break their tie by jumping again over the course, this time with the height and spread of the obstacles increased. This is known as a "jump off."

As a matter of interesting comparison, the scoring of the same performances under FEI rules is shown in the last column. The seven horses with clean performances (no faults) would jump again over the course with the height and spread of the obstacles increased. In the event of equality of faults on the second jump off, time would determine the winner.

In the various A.H.S.A. zones, the winning of a specified number of blue ribbons is required to qualify for the final ride-off at a specified show near the end of the season.

Prescribed tests and courses are provided for each of the five competitions: (a) Saddle horse seat, (b) Hunting seat, (c) Stock saddle seat, (d) P.H.A. dressage, (e) U.S.E.T. combined test.

THE MACLAY—This name is applied to the A.S.P.C.A. (American Society for the Prevention of Cruelty to Animals) horsemanship event. It is called the Maclay because the trophy was donated by the late Alfred B. Maclay. It is open to juniors who have not reached their eighteenth birthday. The competition is over eight jumps, not over three feet in height, and is judged on performance over the fences and on seat and hands. The winner of the final is not eligible for further participation.

HIGH SCORE AWARDS—To encourage participation at recognized shows, in nearly all divisions and in several sections, the A.H.S.A. offers some 23 high score awards. The award is given to the horse which scores the highest number of points in its classification at regular member shows from December 1 through November 30. Points range from 12 for a primary championship to 1 point for eighth place.

PROTESTS—Protests may be made by exhibitors concerning an alleged violation of a rule or condition of a class. The protest must be in writing, signed and addressed to the Secretary of the show, accompanied by a deposit of $25. The judges' decision is not protestable unless it is alleged to be in violation of the rules. Either party to a protest may appeal the decision of the Show Committee to the Enforcement Committee.

A GUIDE FOR HORSE SHOW MANAGERS, OFFICERS AND COMMITTEES

WHAT IS EXPECTED

by EXHIBITORS—

Classes that appeal. Competent and fair judges. Interesting, but not over-difficult courses. Sufficient prize money fairly distributed among first and other places. Adequate stabling. Comfort—Refreshment and toilet facilities. Facilities—Blacksmith, forage, bedding, tack supplies. Entertainment. Accurate time schedule and classes run on time. No conflicts in classes. Friendly attitude and feeling of welcome from officers and committee. Large course-diagrams posted at the In Gate and in the stable area. Doctor and ambulance on the grounds. Schooling area and schooling facilities. Van parking on, or near, the show grounds.

by Spectators—
Ample room to see all events. Boxes available—reserved and preserved for subscribers to them. Parking spaces available—reserved and preserved for those who purchase them. Programs readily available—(Places to obtain them announced). Adequate toilet facilities. Knowledge of what's going on—(Informative announcements). Refreshment available.

by Officials—(That they will:)
Be well-housed, entertained and looked after. Be made to feel welcome and important. Know what they have to do, and when. Have transportation (and suitable escort) always available. Receive remuneration for their travelling expenses and an appropriate fee or present. Chairs and refreshment in a committee stand. Have distinguishing badges.

by the Committee (That each:)
Will be given specific, well defined and reasonable responsibilities. Will be permitted to carry out the assigned responsibilities—within the general framework and objectives—as each sees fit with a minimum of interference and direction. May expect full cooperation from other committee people and officers. Will have the "tools" and money needed available. Will have ready access to the President and other officers and may count on their assistance, advice and encouragement. Will report progress to the President at periodic intervals. Will have plans for follow-up.

In view of the foregoing expectations—the Show Management should plan and direct its activities to have and build a reputation for:

A smooth operation—on time, no conflicts, no confusion. Sound judging. Adequate facilities. Large entries (well filled classes). Good entertainment and fun. Friendly, relaxed happy atmosphere.

91

THE HUNT—When hounds attempt to find and pursue a live fox, it is a **fox hunt.**

When hounds are put on a prepared "line" on which a natural or artificial scent has been dragged, it is a **drag hunt.**

Cubbing is early, pre-season hunting. Its primary purpose is the training of young hounds to hunt fox—pick up the scent, travel together, obey the huntsman's voice and horn, become used to the work and routine of hunting. The term is imported from England where Cubbing is primarily the Blooding of young hounds and the scattering of fox cubs.

To **cast** hounds means to spread them out in a predetermined manner in search of the scent, usually when it has been lost. Usually hounds are cast by the Huntsman, but, frequently, they cast themselves in search of the fox's "line."

A **check** is an interruption of the line (chase) caused by hounds losing the scent.

Drawing a covert means directing and urging the hounds into a small patch of woods where it is expected the fox will be found and chased into open country.

Holding up cubs (during the cubbing season) means surrounding a covert with a staff and field to prevent the fox cubs running out, and, if they attempt to come out, to drive them back so that the young hounds find and kill. Foxes or cubs that do go away are not run. This practice is more prevalent in England than in the United States.

The usual **positions** of the various members of the **hunt staff** when they take hounds to and from a meet should be as follows: Huntsman leading, followed by hounds flanked by Whippers-in, then the Master followed by the Field Master and the Field.

When drawing a covert, the usual **positions** of the members of the **hunt staff** are generally: The Huntsman (or the Master, if he hunts his hounds) with his hounds in the covert near the center, the Whippers-in on either side of him near the edge of the covert so that they may view the fox away and the Master (if he does not hunt his hounds) or the Field Master outside the covert holding up the field.

If there is occasion to lower more than one fence rail, lower the bottom rail first.

THE FOX—A male fox is called a **dog** fox. A **vixen** is a female fox. **Cubs** are young foxes.

Nicknames given the fox by fox hunters include: Reynard, Uncle Remus, Old Charlie, Gentleman Charles, Charles James—the last three after an 18th-Century politician, Charles James Fox. Chaucer refers to him as "Dan Russell."

There are two general types of foxes in the United States—**red** and

gray. The red fox is native to the northeastern United States and Canada, the gray fox more to the south. English (red) foxes were imported to the Eastern Shore of Maryland in 1730 and spread widely. Red and gray foxes are now found in all but desert areas of the U. S. and Canada. The red and gray fox do not interbreed. Color variations of the red fox include the black, the silver and the cross (named for the dark cross on its back). The red fox is found in Europe, Asia and Africa. The gray fox occurs only in North America; it is the only fox that can actually climb trees. Foxes live from ten to twelve years.

The **mask** is the fox's head.

MASK

PAD

BRUSH

The **brush** is the fox's tail.

The **pad** is the fox's paw.

Traditionally, from among those of the Field present at a "kill," the Master awards the fox's **mask** to one of the gentlemen present (frequently a visitor), the **brush** to one of the ladies, and a **pad** each to others present, frequently children.

The **chape** (pronounced "chap") or the **feathers** is the cluster of white hairs at the end of a fox's tail.

A **den**, or **earth** is the fox's abode.

A **covert** (pronounced "cover") is a small wood, thicket, underbrush or similar place where foxes are sheltered and are apt to be found.

Gone to ground refers to a hunted fox getting into an underground den or culvert before hounds can get to him.

Stopping the earth refers to closing or blocking the entrance to a hole leading to a fox's den.

A **straight necked** fox is one which runs in a straight line for a long distance without resorting to trickery to throw the hounds off his line.

A **breast high scent** is one that is particularly good (strong). Scent is apt to be good when there is a gentle steady wind and the fox runs up-wind; when the barometer is steady or a little on the high side, when it is slightly damp, when frost is coming in; on grassland opposed to plowed land; early in the morning, when the ground is apt to be warmer than the air.

DOWNWIND

UP WIND

Down-wind means the fox is running in the direction the wind is blowing—with the wind.

Up-wind means the fox is running against the wind.

HOUNDS—In the U. S. four breeds of hounds are used for hunting in packs: **English, American, Crossbreed** and **Penn-Marydel.**

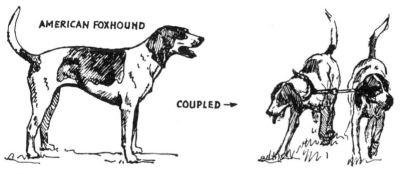

AMERICAN FOXHOUND

COUPLED →

The **American** fox hound differs from the **English** largely in these respects: He has a louder and deeper bay (cry) and uses it more often and freely when on the line of a fox; he has a better nose for the scent; he is lighter and smaller; he has a "hare" foot (as against the "cat" foot of the English hound). These characteristics of the American hound are suited well to the hilly, wooded country of the American countryside, the rough going and comparatively dry climate.

To train young hounds, they are usually **coupled** to older hounds. The couples or couplings are collars joined by metal links.

The **number** of hounds are referred to as so many **couples,** e.g., ten hounds would be referred to as five couples, eleven hounds as five and a half couples. In practice the s is usually dropped.

The most important **attributes** of a good fox hound are:

A **good nose** (ability to follow a scent)—hounds are born with, or inherit this, but the ability can be sharpened by training and hunting.

97

Speed—Depends upon scent. "A hound is no faster than his nose."

Stamina—Largely a matter of good conformation and condition.

Obedience—The willingness to hunt with a pack, respect the huntsmen's horn and voice is affected by disposition and temperament, but is largely a matter of training.

Usually hounds are divided for hunting into **fox hounds** and **drag hounds**, but sometimes the same hounds hunt fox and follow a dragged scent.

Where a hunt has a large pack, frequently the male hounds are hunted together (**the dog pack**) and on other days, the female hounds (**the bitch pack**).

Hounds in their first season of hunting are known as **young entry**.

Hounds' **ears** are frequently marked to show their breeding and ownership.

The **dewlap** is the pendulous fold of skin under the hound's neck.

Hackles are the long hairs on the back of the hound's neck.

The fox hound's **bay** or **cry**, when working on a scent, is referred to variously as: **giving tongue, speaking, honoring the line** and as **music**.

Blooding hounds means encouraging them to break up their fox after they have caught him so that they will be more keen for the chase.

Roading hounds means to exercise them along a road or cross country at slow gaits. The hunt staff may be mounted or on foot.

Walking (putting hounds out at walk) means turning young hounds over to members of the hunt or farmers, for care and exercise until they are ready to be trained and used for hunting.

THE HUNTER (the horse)—The Hunter is not a distinct breed of horse. Actually, any horse that follows hounds cross country over fences is a hunter. Usually, however, they are Thoroughbreds or have a large infusion of Thoroughbred blood.

The **height** of hunters, for adults, is usually 16 to 16.3 hands. They range in **weight** usually from 1100 to 1250 pounds. A lightweight hunter carries up to 165 lbs.; a middleweight up to 185 lbs., and a heavyweight up to 205 lbs.

During the hunting season, hunters are usually clipped, except for their legs and often the saddle area. The legs are not clipped in order to provide protection and because the legs do not sweat.

A **red ribbon** on a horse's tail means that he is a **kicker**—beware.

A hunter's mane is usually **braided**—in even numbers for mares, odd for geldings.

Chief **characteristics** of a good hunter are:

Reliability in jumping all types of obstacles, especially strange ones.

"Honest" jumper, jumping in stride and off hocks in trappy places.
Surefootedness across country of all kinds.
A good stride and speed (way of going).
Comfortable gaits.
Good manners (calm, even temperament and disposition).
Endurance—physical soundness and good conformation.

TACK—The hunting **bridle** has a plain leather brow band and a caves-

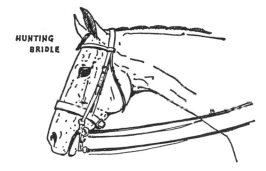

HUNTING
BRIDLE

son nose band. The weight varies according to the bit used, but usually it weighs about 3 lbs.

The **bit** is a snaffle with laced reins, a Pelham (generally of the "Tom Thumb" or short shank variety) with double reins not laced, or a bit and bridoon ("double" or "full" bridle) double and not laced.

Reins are (preferably) sewn to the bit or attached with studs, not buckles. Rubber reins are not used.

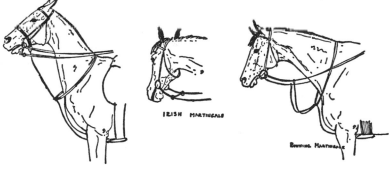

IRISH MARTINGALE

RUNNING MARTINGALE

STANDING MARTINGALE

Martingales are of either the "Standing" or "Running" variety. There is also an Irish "Martingale" which simply couples the reins together to prevent them flying over the horse's head in taking high bank jumps.

The **saddle** is of the type that is referred to as "English" or "Flat." The flaps of the saddle may be relatively straight or of the forward seat variety. The underside is most usually lined with leather, but sometimes with cloth. It is heavy and rugged. The weight varies according to construction, size and age, but it usually weighs about 16 lbs.

Stirrup Irons are large, workmanlike and well polished.

Girths most generally used are leather—Folded, Lonsdale, Balding and Fitzwilliam.

The **billet guards** under the saddle flaps are pulled down to cover the girth buckles.

HUNTING BREASTPLATE, FLASK AND SADDLE

HUNTING SADDLE WITH SANDWICH CASE

A hunting **breastplate** is frequently used to prevent the saddle slipping to the rear. It is a leather strap encircling the horse's neck and attached to the saddle by a strap to the girth under his belly and two small straps near the pommel of the saddle.

The **sandwich case** is carried on the off side of the cantle.

The **flask** is carried on the near side of the pommel.

THE HUNT STAFF—The Hunt Staff consists of the **Master of Fox Hounds (MFH)**; the **huntsman** (unless the Master hunts the hounds), usually a professional—if not a professional, he is referred to as the Honorary Huntsman; two or more **whippers-in** (frequently referred to as **whips**)—either professional or honorary; a **field master**. The Honorary Secretary is an important member of the hunt, but not technically a member of the Hunt Staff.

Master and Huntsman carry a short, straight, metal **horn**, usually between the first and second buttons of their field coat, or in a leather saddle case. Some Southern hunts still retain the cow horn.

The Huntsman carries **wire cutters** and a **pocket knife** on his saddle. The Whippers-in carry a **set of couples** on the off side of their saddles and a spare **stirrup leather** outside of their coats over the right shoulder and under the left arm, buckled in front with the point of the strap down.

All members of the Hunt Staff carry **hunting whips.**

The term **the master carries the horn** means that the Master himself hunts the hounds rather than employing a professional huntsman.

THE FIELD—The **field** are all of the mounted members at a hunt meeting other than the Hunt Staff. They are composed of members of the hunt, subscribers, landowners and their invited guests.

The Field is usually controlled by a **field master.** The Field must adhere strictly to the Field Master's instructions and be careful not to get ahead of him except on his direction.

It is important that all members of the Field are **properly turned out. (See DRESS.)**

IF YOU VIEW A FOX
WITHIN SIGHT OF
MEMBER OF HUNT STAFF

ETIQUETTE—**Greet the Master** on arrival at the meet by raising your hat and saying, "Good morning, Master." When the day's sport is over, **thank the Master**, the Huntsman and the Field Master for your day's sport.

Be careful not to jump a fence if there is danger of **harming a hound.**

If hounds come upon you from the rear, say, "Ware Hounds" (for "Beware").

If a member of the Hunt Staff wishes to pass, say, "Way for the Huntsman"; (Make way).

Give the person ahead of you **room to fall.**

When you are headed for a panel, jump that one and **do not cross over.** A **panel** is a jumpable section of fence.

When riding through the woods, brush by branches and twigs (and duck under them)—**do not hold** a branch or twig; if you do it will snap back in the face of the rider behind.

If you **view a fox in sight** of a member of the Hunt Staff, say nothing, but remove your hat and with it **point in** the direction the fox has gone.

When in the vicinity of hounds, or hounds are passing, turn your horse's head toward them to avoid the possibility of kicking.

Remain **quiet** at covert-side and at check avoid disturbing any stock at pasture.

DRESS—The origin of the **scarlet hunting coat** is somewhat obscure. The version most generally accepted by hunting men and those who have made a study of the subject, is that scarlet was used by early fox hunters to distinguish themselves from the harriers and stag hunters who traditionally wore green and sometimes blue or gray. Scarlet was probably popular because of the predominance of this color in the English military uniform. Also, Henry II decreed stag hunting a royal sport and that members of the hunt should wear the royal livery— scarlet. Previous to the ascendancy of fox hunting, the hunting uniforms, as a rule, were tailored in the colors of the Master's livery.

The term **Pink**, so frequently used to describe the scarlet hunting coat is *not* slang for scarlet as is generally assumed; it has nothing to do with color. The term derived from the popularity of a fashionable gentlemen's tailor by the name of Pink, famous for his fine sporting turnouts early in the 19th century. The term Pink appears in writing at the time but was little used prior to the advent of the tailor. In any event, Mr. Pink seems to have emphasized and popularized his name among the hunting set of his time—and since!

The term **ratcatcher** refers to informal hunting dress as opposed to formal hunting attire—a tweed jacket, an ordinary felt hat or cap, brown boots, etc.

DRESS in the hunting field is a matter of custom which may vary somewhat in different hunting countries—but, as a rule, the following is customary and considered correct:

In America, **Scarlet** is worn only by gentlemen members of the hunt awarded their buttons and colors by the Master. (In rare instances, ladies who are Masters of Fox Hounds have worn scarlet.) Other than scarlet, the correct color of the coat worn at formal meetings is **black**. While scarlet is traditionally associated with fox hunting and is most universally worn, in some instances, the formal hunting coat worn by members who have been awarded their colors is other than scarlet, such as blue, gray, yellow, etc. This, however, is more common in England where these other colors have been handed down from the livery of an early Master.

The **black velvet hunting cap** is worn only by members of the Hunt Staff, the Honorary Secretary, former Masters of Fox Hounds and children.

The **ribbons** on the back of the hunting cap are conventionally worn hanging down below the cap by professionals—up by others.

The **breeches** are traditionally and nearly always white and of heavy material—not cotton polo breeches. Some hunts, however, prescribe, as uniform for their members, rust or buff color breeches.

The **boot garter**, for men in scarlet, should be the same color as the breeches—therefore, generally white. Women, however, wear black patent leather boot garters. Men wearing black coats, also wear black boot garters.

Formal hunting boots for men are black with tan or russet tops. These should not be worn with the black hunting jacket. In this case, the boots are black without tops. Women's formal hunting boots are black with black patent leather tops.

Plain heavy **spurs**—with moderate shanks—should be worn with formal attire.

Gentlemen wearing scarlet—who are not members of the Hunt Staff —wear a **silk top hat** with a scarlet cord. Others wear **bowlers** (derby) with a black cord. Women wear a bowler with a black cord. (As previously stated, children generally wear hunting caps.)

The **stock pin** should be plain and worn horizontally (in order to avoid being stuck by it in the event of a fall).

Following is a memorandum on **correct hunting attire** circulated to its members by a long and well established New York hunt:

CORRECT HUNTING ATTIRE
(During the Regular Season)

GENTLEMEN:

Those invited by the Masters to wear the Hunt buttons and colors:

Top hat with scarlet cord
Scarlet coat with metal Hunt buttons, and Hunt colors on collar
Yellow vest
White Hunting stock with horizontal plain pin
White twill breeches
Black boots with tan tops
White boot garters
Blunt spurs (no rowels)
Hunting whip

Those who have not yet been invited to wear the Hunt colors:
Black bowler (derby) with black cord
Black coat
Yellow or tattersall waistcoat
Hunting stock with horizontal plain pin
Grey, rust or buff breeches
Plain black boots, no tops and black boot garters
Blunt spurs

Only members of the Hunt Staff, former masters of recognized hunts and Juniors may wear hunting caps.

Tan top boots are worn only with scarlet coats. Patent leather tops are under no circumstances worn by gentlemen.

Professionals, whether subscribers or "capping," wear the same attire as the other members of the Hunt—grooms and second horsemen wear rat-catcher.

LADIES:

Those invited by the Masters to wear the Hunt buttons and colors:
Black bowler (derby) with black cord.
Black coat with colors on collar, black bone Hunt buttons
Yellow vest with metal Hunt buttons
White hunting stock with horizontal plain pin
Canary or buff twill breeches
Black boots with black patent leather tops, blunt spurs

Those who have not yet been invited to wear the Hunt colors:
The same, with the exception of colors, and buttons on coat and vest, which will be plain black bone, for coat, plain metal for vest.

JUNIORS:

Those invited by the Masters to wear the Hunt buttons and colors:
Same as ladies, with the exception of plain boots for boys, and hunting caps in all cases.

Those who have not yet been invited to wear the Hunt buttons and colors:
Black hunting cap
Black coat
Yellow vest
Hunting stock with horizontal plain pin
Grey, buff or canary breeches
Black boots, plain for boys, patent leather tops for girls
Blunt spurs

ALL:

Gloves—tan leather, or, in wet weather, yellow or white string, will be worn.

LORE

MR. JORROCKS is a famous mythical character who freely dispensed good advice on hunting in cockney. He was created by the noted English hunting author, R. S. SURTEES.
JOHN PEEL is a famous Old English foxhunting song composed by JOHN WOODCOCK GRAVES.
For origin of the term PINK see "Dress" in this section.
It is traditional to pull on the LEFT BOOT first.

ORGANIZED HUNTS

The governing body of foxhunting in the United States is the MASTERS OF FOXHOUNDS ASSOCIATION OF AMERICA.
In the United States there are approximately 100 hunts recognized by the Masters of Foxhounds Association. A list of these is published annually by *The Chronicle*.

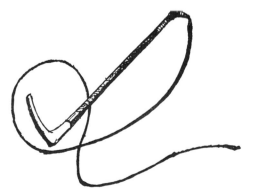

Although not strictly activities connected with horses, (there are no mounted beagle or basset packs in the U.S.), pack beagling and bassetting have been recognized in recent years as important primers to fox hunting, particularly for Pony Club children. Some of its advantages as an introduction to fox hunting are very similar procedure, excellent visibility, proximity to hounds and hence a really good view of hound work, lack of worry about riding well and jumping fences, and lack of expense.

THE HUNT—Packs of beagles and bassets in the United States pursue two quarries: hares and cottontail rabbits.

There are (1959) 19 packs of beagles recognized by the National Beagle Club in the United States, and 6 packs of bassets also recognized by the National Beagle Club, all east of the Mississippi. These beagles and bassets are registered with the American Kennel Club and many beagle and basset packs compete in their own pack trials and in hound shows. The American Kennel Club is at 221 Fourth Ave., New York City.

Besides beagles registered from packs, there are also a great number of individually owned and hunted beagles which compete in single hound trials or snowshoe hare trials for field championships, or are used for gunning. The above, plus a large number of beagles which compete in dog shows for bench championships, or are kept as pets, accounts for their having the largest registration of any dog in the American Kennel Club in recent years.

Because of the two types of championships offered to registered beagles by the A.K.C., American beagles have been diversified into bench type, with lots of style and little thought of hunting, and field type, with keen hunting ability and little thought of conformation. Pack beagles are somewhat in the middle as the ideal is to have a uniform, good type pack, which hunts hard, well and closely.

Bassets, to date, have not suffered from this type of diversification, largely because they are not as popular as the beagle.

Beagle and basset packs do not drag hunt (run an artificial scent).

THE QUARRIES—**The hare**—Two varieties of hare are hunted by packs:

The **European hare**—25–27 inches long, ears 5 inches, weight 7–12 pounds, brown, but may have black-tipped ears and tail like a jackrabbit—native to parts of New Jersey, New York and Canada.

The **Blacktail Jackrabbit**—17–21 inches long, ears 6–7 inches, weight 3–7 pounds, light brown with black-tipped ears and tail—the common American hare—native to the west, but introduced to the east and hunted in Pennsylvania, New Jersey, New York and Connecticut.

The **European hare**, as compared with the **Jackrabbit**, usually gets

109

HARE (*About 2 ft. long*)

COTTONTAIL RABBIT

up ahead of hounds, runs longer points, and gallops rather than leaps. The Jackrabbit often springs up from its "form" in the midst of hounds or after they have passed over it, makes frequent high leaps, and "squats" frequently throughout the hunt. Both generally run in large circles.

Male hares are called **bucks** or **jacks**; females are called **does**. Young hares are called **leverets**. A nickname given to hares is **puss**. A hare's head is called a **mask**. A hare's tail is called a **scut**. A hare's foot is called a **pad**.

The mask or a pad may be awarded by the Master to a deserving member of the field at a kill.

Hares are always referred to as **she**.

Leverets are born in open fields, with their eyes open, and covered with hair. They are left separated in a field, the doe visiting and feeding each one in turn.

The hare's **enemies** are owls, hawks, coyotes, foxes, dogs, gunners, cars, and weed-killing poisons.

A hare's **form** (lair) is a shallow scoop in the ground where a hare crouches, perfectly camouflaged, ready to spring out with a good push-off.

To **get up a hare** means to surprise one into running.

Squat means for a hare to crouch low, virtually invisible in grass or plow, but not necessarily in a form.

To **take to covert** (pronounced "cover") means that a hare enters heavy growth or woods to shake off pursuing hounds.

Double-back means that a hare runs back on her trail for a way and leaves it at an angle, sometimes with a long leap.

Running through foil means that a hare obliterates her scent by running through manure, fertilizer, etc.

The Cottontail Rabbit—The **Eastern** cottontail—14–17 inches long, ears 2½–3 inches long, weight 2–4 pounds, brown with white cottony tail—is a resident of heavy brush, hedgerows and forests. It may nest

BEAGLE   BASSETT

and feed in the open but must have heavy cover nearby. It is a devious runner, twisting and turning, staying generally in covert, and resorting to many tricks.

Young cottontails are born on the surface of the ground in nests, usually not in burrows, although all cottontails resort to burrows as hiding places. They are almost hairless, eyes closed, and helpless. Their enemies are dogs, cats, foxes, owls, hawks, snakes, gunners, cars, and weed-killing poisons.

When differentiating between hares and rabbits, think of "long legged, leaping hares" and "short legged, running rabbits."

HOUNDS—In the United States, there is only **one breed** of beagles, but they come in two sizes: under 13" and 13–15". (The English limit is 16".)

Bassets are also **one breed** but there is no classification by size.

Young hounds are **coupled** to older ones to train them to stay in the pack.

Young hounds that are going to hunt hare are usually trained to hunt cottontails first. The theory is that since a cottontail leaves a fainter scent and more devious trail, any hound that can run a cottontail can surely run a hare. Also, hunting cottontails is slower and less apt to discourage a young puppy; in addition, it teaches them not to be afraid to enter a covert.

The number of beagles or bassets in a pack is referred to as so many "couples," e.g., nine hounds are referred to as 4½ couples.

The attributes of a good pack beagle or basset include:

A good nose—keen scenting ability.

Stamina—ruggedness resulting from good conformation.

Steadiness—an even disposition, not likely to be rattled or to fault.

Drive—enthusiasm for the kill.

Voice—pleasing, preferably loud and used only on scent.

Obedience—a willingness to pack up, share team-work with other pack members, and respond to huntsman and horn. It is, of course, promoted by sound and constant training.

Beagles and bassets are always referred to as "hounds" (not dogs). Their tails are called **sterns** and the loose hairs up the back of them are called a **brush**.

Young beagles in their first year of pack work are called **young entry**.

The **ideal beagle**, regardless of size grouping, should have:

A slightly domed, generous head with long, low-set ears, large dark, pleading eyes, a medium-length square-cut muzzle with level jaws, and large open nostrils.

A neck that is of medium length and strong without being loaded with skin folds; sloping, clean, muscular shoulders; a short strong back; well-sprung ribs and hind quarters that are well let down at the stifle as well as being muscular.

He should have plenty of leg-bone for his weight and close firm feet. His stern should be set on moderately high, have ample brush and be carried gaily. His coat should be close and hard and his color may be any true hound color, which includes white, lemon and white, red and white, and blue-ticked as well as the predominant black, tan and white.

His general appearance, to quote the American Kennel Club beagle standard, is that of "a miniature foxhound, solid and big for his inches, with the wear-and-tear look of the hound that can last in the chase and follow his quarry to the death."

As to **bassets**:

Since they were developed in France for hunting game in thick covert and for trailing wounded game slowly, the emphasis in their structure is on lowness and strength. The basset's general appearance is a docile, somewhat awkward hound of great dignity. In action, he is surprisingly agile and every inch the workman.

The **ideal basset** should have a large head with narrow skull, heavy flews, and forehead wrinkled to the eyes. His nose should be free from snipiness and his teeth should meet evenly. His ears should be long and velvety, set low on his head, and his eyes dark brown and deeply sunk. His neck should be powerful in heavy dewlaps and set on sloping shoulders. His chest should be deep, back long and straight, and well-sprung ribs. His forelegs should be short, heavy in bone with a crooked knee, but never out at the elbow. He should have round-as-an-apple quarters, be well let down in the hock, and his feet should be massive with weight well-distributed on the toes. His stern should be carried upright, his coat should be firm, and his color any true hound color.

THE HUNT STAFF—The Hunt Staff consists of the **Master of Beagles or Bassets (M.B.)**, the **huntsman** (unless the Master hunts the hounds), two or more **whippers-in**, referred to as **whips**, the **field master**, the Honorary Secretary, and the Honorary Treasurer. If the Huntsman is not a professional, he is referred to as the Honorary Huntsman; if a Whipper-In is not a professional, he is referred to as an Honorary Whipper-In.

The Huntsman carries a horn, somewhat smaller than a fox-hunting horn, either copper or silver, and usually a whip.

The Whippers-In carry whips which differ from foxhunting whips in that they have an ash-stock handle instead of a leather covered one, are straight instead of having a hook in the end for opening gates, and the lash is shorter.

THE FIELD—The **field** is composed of subscribers and members of the hunt and their guests, or—if the pack is not a subscription pack—the guests of the Master. The field is obliged to follow the Field Master at all times so as not to get in the way of the hounds and Hunt Staff or cause undue damage to landowners.

BEAGLERS

DRESS—The Hunt Staff wear a soft black velvet hunting cap, white stock with plain gold stock pin—or, in some instances, white shirt with white tie; a field green or other color coat with the collar in the Hunt color, and brass or black buttons with Hunt insignia; white trousers, or white breeches or shorts with green or other color stockings, (ladies wear short white skirts with green or other color stockings or gaiters); white sneakers or brown leather shoes, and brown leather gloves. The Huntsman (usually) and Whippers-In carry beagling whips.

113

Subscribers to or members of the hunt may wear the livery (green or other color coat) with hunt collar only by invitation of the Master. Such invitations are given to those who have shown interest, knowledge, and enthusiasm for the sport over a considerable period of time.

Others in the field may wear any neat, clean, appropriate outdoor clothing.

ETIQUETTE—Be properly turned out, whether a member of the Hunt Staff or the field.

Greet the Master and the Field Master at the meet. Introduce your guests to them and see that the "capping fee" is paid. When the day's sport is over, **thank the Master**, the Huntsman, and the Field Master for the day's sport.

Stay behind the Field Master at all times.

Be moderately quiet in the field and absolutely quiet at a check so as not to disturb hounds.

Climb fences at the post, so as not to break rails in the middle of the panel; close gates; avoid new or soft lawns, new seeding, and all crops not yet harvested.

Notify the Master if you cause any damage so that he can rectify it or pay for it, since hunting exists only through the courtesy of the landowners.

Avoid disturbing any stock at pasture.

Do **not** "halloo" (pronounced "holler") if you view a hare—get on her line, raise your cap, and point in the direction she has gone. Halloos generally only excite, distract, and rattle hounds. If you are far from the Huntsman and hounds, e.g., behind the field, and view a hare, you should get on the line, point in the direction she has gone, and call "Tally-Ho" or the less often used old English "So-Ho" until either a Whipper-In or the Huntsman sees and understands your signal. Care should be taken not to get hounds' heads up. Do not expect the Huntsman to bring hounds to your view. It may be a fresh hare in his opinion or he may want hounds to hunt the line without being lifted. However, he does appreciate knowledge of every hare in the vicinity.

If a hare bolts through the field, stand stock still so as not to turn the hare. After she has passed, continue to stand still with head turned in her direction until hounds are well away to avoid confusing them. Then fall in behind the Field Master.

Do not try to turn a hare or rabbit; you would only confuse the quarry and the scent as well.

Do not follow a beagle or basset hunt in a car—the fumes destroy scent and landowners generally object to traffic on their lanes and driveways.

GLOSSARY—**so-ho**—the equivalent of "Tally-Ho" in foxhunting—alerting the Hunt Staff that a hare has been sighted.

view—hounds see a hare or rabbit.

brought to their noses—hounds lose sight of a viewed hare and have to run by scent.

hit off the line—hounds have recovered the scent after a check.

pick a check—the same.

at fault—hounds have lost the scent.

feather—a hound works a faint scent, not sure enough to speak, but waves its stern rapidly.

skirter—a hound that cuts corners rather than follow the exact line.

riot—to hunt anything other than legitimate quarry; a fault.

dwell—when a hound does not drive forward on the line; a fault.

babble—when a hound gives tongue without reason; a fault.

heel—when a hound runs a scent the wrong way; a fault.

chop—when hounds kill a hare or rabbit without having hunted her.

all on—a Whipper-In's report to the Huntsman that all hounds are counted and present.

STEEPLECHASE—A steeplechase is a horse race over brush obstacles on a prescribed course. The term is sometimes used broadly to mean any kind of race over obstacles of whatever nature—on a course or cross-country. The term "Steeplechase" originated in the 18th century when it was usual for the sporting gentry to race cross-country from a designated point a distance of approximately four miles to "Yon church steeple"—the only reference point clearly visible on the horizon. Hence, such a race was termed a steeplechase. These point-to-point races, if the desirable shortest course was followed, naturally required jumping fences. Ultimately, the majority of races over fences were confined to smaller areas, prescribed courses and more or less standard obstacles—with a church steeple no longer required for reference. The name, however, stuck.

POINT-TO-POINT—A point-to-point is actually a race across natural country and natural obstacles from one specified point to another (and sometimes return) over any route the rider chooses to follow. Today, however, the term generally refers to a jumping race over natural country but between a flagged course.

HUNT RACE MEETING—A series of races usually over brush, hurdle and timber, under the auspices of a recognized Hunt and governed by National Steeplechase and Hunt Association rules.

HURDLE RACE—Prior to 1950, a hurdle race was one over a prescribed course in which the obstacles were "sheep hurdles," panels of light wood fencing with brush set in them, inclined "away" at an angle of 15° from the perpendicular. Since that time, hurdle fences are smaller size replicas of the brush type of fence, a frame of wood filled with cedar and brushed with the same material on the "take off" side. The height of these is 4' 4" whereas a regular brush fence is 5' 2" high.

NUMBER AND LOCATION—The greatest number of jumping races of all kinds is held in New York; Virginia is second, Pennsylvania third.

The greatest number of hunt and point-to-point races occurs in Virginia; Pennsylvania is second, Maryland third.

HURDLE

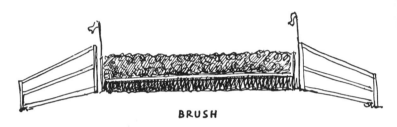

BRUSH

OBSTACLES (FENCES)—The obstacles in jumping races are usually **timber** (post and rail), **brush** (hedge) and **hurdles** (described in a preceding paragraph). There are substantially more steeplechase races over brush and hurdles than over timber.

The height of the usual steeplechase obstacles in the United States (including hurdles) is from 4' 4" to over 5 feet. (However, on some big brush courses, the obstacles are six feet high.) Brush is usually 3 to 3½ feet wide.

A water jump is prescribed as being a minimum of 6 feet wide and 2 feet deep with a fence not less than 2 feet high on the take-off side.

Each of the obstacles on a steeplechase course is flagged. A small red or blue flag indicates the inside of the course—that it should be jumped with the flag on the rider's left. Small white flags are placed on the opposite side of the obstacle (indicating the outside of the course—that it should be jumped with the flag on the rider's right).

LENGTH OF COURSES—A steeplechase run at a racing establishment or track is usually 2 to 2½ miles. Hunt race meetings over natural country are frequently about 4 miles. For hunters, the minimum is 2½ miles over brush and 3½ miles over timber. In steeplechases, at least four obstacles per mile are required.

RIDERS—Steeplechase riders use a much longer stirrup than flat race jockeys and ride more in the saddle than the former. Steeplechase riders are required to wear a light, but strong, plastic skull cap under the silk.

Riders other than professionals are generally referred to as "Mr."

WEIGHT—The **minimum weight** permitted in any steeplechase is 130 pounds and, in races exclusively for hunters, the minimum is 145 pounds. Amateur steeplechase riders in a hunt race frequently weigh in up to 170 pounds and quite generally from 150 to 160. However, except when an amateur rider is up, a horse may not carry more than five pounds over the prescribed weight.

THE STEEPLECHASE HORSE—The steeplechaser is not a distinct breed —most of them, however, are Thoroughbreds.

Horses are not permitted to run in a steeplechase until August 1 of the year in which they are three years old. The age of steeplechase horses in top competition ranges all the way from 3 to 10 years.

The greatest number of steeplechase horses are produced, in order, in Kentucky, Virginia and Maryland. Most of the imported horses come from England and Ireland.

The length of a racing horse's leap over an average obstacle is about 20 feet.

A good steeplechaser will cover a two mile brush or hurdle course in about three minutes and forty-five seconds and a four mile course over timber or big brush in about 8½ to 9 minutes.

Many good steeplechasers have had experience on the flat as two and three-year olds. On the other hand, horses originally trained for steeplechasing and unsuccessful as steeplechasers, have generally had little success on the flat. There are a few notable exceptions—one being, **Azucar**, originally trained as a steeplechaser, who won the first running of the Santa Anita handicap.

Steeplechase horses are usually handicapped—as are flat horses— for age, sex, apprentice or inexperienced riders, and for past performance.

COURSES—In the United States there are a number of timber as well as brush and hurdle courses and races.

In England the courses are almost entirely brush; there are also a few hurdle races.

Prior to 1958 William duPont's **Fox Catcher Farm** course at Fair Hill, Maryland is reputed to have had the highest brush obstacles in the world—they averaged six feet.

THE MARYLAND HUNT CUP—The Maryland Hunt Cup course at Glyndon, Maryland is reputed to have the biggest timber obstacles.

121

A LIVERPOOL

The course, over natural hunting country, is about four miles. The fences average about four feet three inches—the highest are four feet ten inches. No rider has been fatally injured in negotiating this course, although several horses have had falls which necessitated destroying them. The trophy for the race is a very much coveted silver cup; there is no purse. One horse, **Blockade**, won the race three times—in 1938, 1939 and 1940—and established the course record of 8 minutes, 44 seconds.

THE GRAND NATIONAL—Perhaps the most famous steeplechase in the world is the **English Grand National** at Aintree, near Liverpool, inaugurated in 1839.

The course is about 4½ miles—exactly 4 miles, 856 yards—and there are 30 obstacles.

The fastest time recorded for this race is 9 minutes, 20 seconds by **Golden Miller** in 1934.

Despite the difficulty of the course, there has been only one fatality (**James Wynne** in 1862).

Two American bred horses have won the English Grand National —**Rubio** (owned by an Englishman) in 1908 and **Battleship** (owned by Mrs. M. du Pont Scott) in 1938. Four American owned horses have won the race—**Sergeant Murphy** (owned by Stephen Sanford) in 1923, **Jack Horner** (owned by A. C. Schwartz) in 1926, **Kellsboro Jack** (owned by Mrs. F. Ambrose Clark) in 1933 and **Battleship**.

Horses running in the Grand National must be six years or more old.

The winners of the Grand National have been predominantly geldings.

Top weight carried in the Grand National is 175 pounds. Minimum is 130.

There is a Grand National steeplechase run at Belmont Park near New York inaugurated in 1899. It is over brush, three miles and an eighth in length.

The Temple Gwathmey run at Belmont Park by the United Hunts Racing Association has the greatest money value for a steeplechase in the United States.

HISTORY—The first jumping race on a regular track in the United States was in 1834 at the Jockey Club track in Washington, D. C.

DEFINITIONS—**Catch weights** refers to a race run without regard to the weight carried.

Liverpool refers to an obstacle composed of an open ditch in front of a high brush fence, generally with a low rail on the take-off side.

Walk-over refers to a situation where only one horse (or several horses belong to a single owner) is ready to start the race at the appointed time.

RULES—The rules permit a rider who has fallen to remount and continue the race—provided he does so in the space between the obstacle he last jumped and the next jump or the last fence and the finish. Likewise, if a rider falls and his horse gets away and is caught by a spectator and returned to him, he may remount and continue the race —provided he remounts in the area described previously.

If an obstacle is broken, other horses are permitted to jump the broken panel and usually do. If a horse runs out at an obstacle or is off course, he may continue the race from the point where he ran out or left the course.

If a rider weighs in overweight after a race, the rider is fined, sus-

STEEPLECHASE
SEAT

pended or ruled out if he is more than two pounds overweight unless it is caused by rain or mud. If a rider weighs in light after a race, his horse is disqualified if he is light over two pounds. Under NO conditions may a horse finish a race with a rider other than the one at the start, although years ago this was permitted under some conditions.

If a horse is second and there is a purse for second place—if the second place horse finishes five minutes or more behind the winner, he does not collect.

RACING SEAT
on the flat

HISTORY—New York State is generally credited with having pioneered organized horse racing in the United States—on the Hempstead Plains on Long Island in the 1660's. This was on a course. In Virginia, there was much "quarter" racing in the early days—a quarter of a mile straight away.

Flat racing owes its rules and customs in large part to Lord George Cavendish–Bentinck, son of the Duke of Portland and owner of the never beaten Crucifix. During the 1840's he devised: (1) The method of starting with a flag. (2) Parading horses in the paddock before a race. (3) The number-board showing runners and riders. (4) The preliminary canter to the post. (5) Insisted on punctuality by jockeys, trainers, owners and officials. (6) Abolished the custom of giving a present to the judge after winning a race.

TRACKS—Tracks in the United States are characteristically sand or natural earth (built on a clay base with a cushion composed of sand and loam). Recently there has been a considerable increase in natural grass turf courses (inside the sand tracks), especially at the larger racing establishments. In England and in Europe the footing—with very few exceptions—is grass turf.

The best known flat racing tracks in the United States are: Belmont, Aqueduct and Saratoga in New York (Saratoga is the oldest race course in the United States still in use—inaugurated in 1864); Churchill Downs in Louisville, Kentucky; Santa Anita in Arcadia near Los Angeles, California; Hialeah near Miami, Florida; Pimlico and Laurel in Maryland; Arlington Park and Washington Park near Chicago, Illinois; the Fair Grounds in New Orleans, Louisiana; Garden State near Camden, New Jersey.

States with the greatest number of tracks (of a mile or more) are: California with 6, Florida and Illinois with 4, Kentucky, Maryland, New Jersey and New York with 3 each.

LARGEST ESTABLISHMENTS—The largest racing and breeding establishments in the United States are: Calumet Farm, Greentree, Maine Chance Farm, Darby Dan Farm, Spendthrift Farm, Claiborne Farm,

Mr. George D. Widener's racing and breeding stables, all in Kentucky, and the Ellsworth Ranch in California and the King Ranch in Texas. In the past, Col. E. R. Bradley's Idle Hour farm turned out four Kentucky Derby winners. At Elmendorf, also in the Kentucky Blue Grass country, stands a bronze, life-size statue of Fair Play, sire of Man o' War. The C. V. Whitney farm in Kentucky has its own horse graveyard, with white headstones commemorating Broomstick, Whisk Broom II, Peter Pan and others. The stallion barn at Almahurst stands on the exact spot where the great Exterminator was foaled. Coldstream Stud, which breeds and sells, but does not race, was the home of the "little red horse," Aristides, winner of the first Kentucky Derby. The enormous King Ranch in Texas has bred and raced such champions as Assault and High Gun. More than 1,500,000 people came to Faraway Farm in Kentucky to visit the incomparable Man o' War, who died in 1947 at the age of twenty-nine.

THE CLASSIC RACES—There are three great races for three-year-olds: 1. Most colorful and popular is **The Kentucky Derby**, 1¼ miles, run on the first Saturday in May at Churchill Downs, in Louisville. The Derby, inaugurated in 1875, is patterned after the classic English Derby at Epsom Downs. The only filly to win the Derby was Regret in 1915. 2. Second of the tests for three-year-old Thoroughbreds is **The Preakness**, at 1 3/16 miles, run on another venerable track, Pimlico, in Baltimore, Maryland. Although the race was inaugurated in 1873, two years before the Derby, it was not run from 1883 to 1890. 3. **The Belmont Stakes**, known as "The Test of the Champion" is at the grueling distance of 1½ miles. Run at Belmont Park, on Long Island, the race dates back to 1867 and is the oldest of the "Triple Crown" events. Its winners are among the all-time greats of American racing. Its first winner was a filly, Ruthless. A second filly, Tanya, won in 1905. Thoroughbreds who accomplish the difficult feat of winning all three of the above are known as "Triple Crown Winners."

The Withers, also run at Belmont, is the oldest and most important stake at one mile, restricted to three-year-olds. It was inaugurated in 1875, when it was won by Aristides, winner of the first Kentucky Derby. Other well known races include: the Santa Anita Handicap near Los Angeles, California; the Garden State Handicap and Garden State Stakes at Garden State Park, New Jersey; the Monmouth Handicap and Sapling Stakes at Monmouth Park, New Jersey; the Washington, D. C., International at Laurel, Maryland; the American Derby at Washington Park near Chicago; the Hopeful Stakes at Saratoga; the Futurity at Belmont Park; the Suburban Handicap at Belmont Park; the Travers at Saratoga, New York (this is the oldest stakes race in the United States —originated in 1864).

DIRECTION—On American tracks, horses run **counterclockwise**. In England and in Europe, horses run both counterclockwise and clockwise.

DISTANCE—**Two year olds** usually race about six furlongs. Starting at three furlongs at the beginning of the season, the distances are gradually increased as the season progresses and may be extended to as much as 1 1/16 miles in November. (A **furlong** is ⅛ of a mile or 220 yards.)

Three year olds usually run up to 1½ miles.

The larger tracks in the United States are generally a mile oval but there are several ½ mile tracks. At the larger tracks there are occasionally "chutes" or straightaways for races up to six and one-half furlongs. Belmont is the only 1½ mile track in the U. S.

TIME—The **record** for a mile in the **United States** is 1 minute 33⅕ seconds. It was set by **Swaps** as a four year old, carrying 128 pounds, in the Argonaut Handicap on June 9, 1956 at Hollywood Park, California.

The **world record** for a mile is 1 minute 32 seconds, set by **Mopsus** on June 22, 1939 at Brighton, England. (The Brighton Track is a straightaway, slightly downhill.) **Swaps'** mile mark of 1:33⅕ is the world record for an oval track.

Earlier records for the mile in the United States are these: In 1800, 1 minute 45½ seconds (**Flying Dutchman**); in 1900, 1 minute 35½ seconds (**Salvator**).

Good time for six furlongs is 1 minute 11 seconds. Good time for a mile and ⅛ is 1 minute 50 seconds; for a mile and ¼, 2 minutes 2 seconds; for a mile and ½, 2 minutes 31 seconds; for 2 miles, about 3 minutes 24 seconds. (These figures are, of course, influenced by type of track and racing conditions.)

PRODUCE—The **greatest number** of Thoroughbreds is foaled (produced) in Kentucky; California is second; and Virginia, third.

RACING TERMS—**Handicap**—Horses are handicapped by carrying additional weight (lead weights added to the saddle). Handicaps are assigned by an impartial "handicapper"—currently usually the Racing Secretary—in consideration of age, sex (fillies and mares are favored) and performance (amount and number of previous winnings).

Allowance race—Weight for age, plus weight penalties for prize money earned.

Stakes—A race in which the entry fees and any added money are divided amongst the winner, second, third and fourth horses.

Sweepstakes—The winner takes all—currently infrequent.

Claiming race—A race in which any of the horses may be bought (claimed) by any other owner of an entry in that meeting for the price posted by the owner prior to the running of the race.

Sprint—Up to 7 furlongs.

Middle distance—Up to 1¼ miles.

Stayer distance—1½ miles and over.

Maiden—A horse which has not won a race.

Place—To come in second (in betting, second or better).

Show—To come in third (in betting, third or better).

Across the board—The horse is bet to win, place and show; that is, come in first, second or third. This type of bet is also known as a "combination ticket." (It is a convenience in placing or collecting a bet, but has no premium value.)

Daily double—A bet that a specified horse in each of the first two races will win. If *both* horses do not win, the bet is lost.

Parlay—To apply an original bet and the winnings on a horse in a succeeding race.

Odds-on—A bet which, if won, will return an amount less than the bet, e.g., one to two—you wager $10 to win $5, collecting, if you win, $15; the $10 you put up and $5 in winnings.

Pari-mutuel—A system of mechanically pooling bets and distributing the total proportionately among the holders of tickets on the winning, second and third horses. The odds, therefore, depend on the amounts bet on the winning, second and third horses. A percentage of the total bet is retained by the State and Track before distribution. The machine which computes the odds is known as a "Totalisator," or "Tote." This method is distinguished from individual bookmaking in which the bookmaker establishes the odds and his percentage.

Garrison finish—A horse coming from behind with a whirlwind burst of speed during the run through the stretch. The term was derived from "Snapper" Garrison's characteristic manner of riding his races.

Produce race—One in which the offspring of specified mares only are eligible—a race for the unborn produce of horses named at the time nominations for the event close.

Breezed under wraps—The rider holding a horse well in hand at a pace slower than he can or would gallop if he were not restrained by his rider.

Rating—To steady a horse—hold him back a little at an even rate of speed up to the final dash so that he will have something left for a strong finish.

Quinella—A wager to select the *first two* horses to finish in a race. The order in which they finish is immaterial.

130

Asterisk * before a horse's name indicates an imported stallion or brood mare.

Names—All Thoroughbred horses must be registered and Jockey Club rules require that no name shall exceed sixteen letters and spaces. Names of famous horses are retired, so that they may never again be used. If a horse is not well known, his name may be picked up and re-used after fifteen years.

Racing Colors—Stables apply for and register their colors with the Jockey Club. Colors may be registered for one year or for life. However, as with names, the colors of famous stables are never given out twice (i.e. the famous green and white of Bradley or the Woodward polkadots).

Pole—Distances on the track are marked at each sixteenth of a mile, by poles. The Finish Pole often is painted with special colors to avoid mishaps like that in the Kentucky Derby of 1956 when Willie Shoemaker on Gallant Man, eased the horse at what he mistook for the finish line—and lost the race.

Dead Heat—When two or more horses cross the finish line with no margin between them. There have been triple dead heats and at least one four-horse dead heat.

Photo-Finish—The finish of a race close enough to require examination of a photograph of the horses passing the finish line before announcing the winner and placing the order of finish.

Ringer—The substitution in a race of one horse for another—illegal and extremely rare. Scandals of many years ago involved horses being painted to disguise their identity.

Plater—An inferior horse; he races for prizes (plate) instead of the big-money stakes.

Plates—The thin and light metal shoes worn by race horses.

Objection—When the "Objection" sign is flashed on the board, it means there has been a protest lodged (most often by one jockey against another) or the stewards have called for an inquiry into the running of the race. Offenses include crossing over in front of another horse, impeding his progress, forcing another horse to go wide, thus making him give up ground, impeding at the start, etc.

FAMOUS HORSES—Many horses have, for a time, had the distinction of being the greatest **money-winning** horses, but since the number of tracks changes over the years and purses become larger, while the dollar is apt to decline, the record changes rather frequently. Several horses have earned over a million dollars during their racing career.

Winners of the **Triple Crown** (Kentucky Derby, Preakness and Belmont Stakes) include **Sir Barton**—1919, **Gallant Fox**—1930, **Omaha**

—1935, **War Admiral**—1937, **Whirlaway**—1941, **Count Fleet**—1943, **Assault**—1946, **Citation**—1948.

Exterminator was known as "Old Bones."

Man o' War was known as "Big Red." He won 20 of his 21 starts.

Phar Lap, an Australian gelding, winner of the Melbourne Cup, arrived in the United States in 1932 as a 5-year-old to race against leading American horses including **Twenty Grand**. He died shortly after a warm-up race on the West Coast.

Kincsem had the longest string of victories known to the turf, winning 54 consecutive races. Her career ended in 1880.

Eclipse (1764–1789) has been called the most famous horse in the history of the Turf. Never beaten, he sired a long line of English winners.

Citation was the first of the "millionaire horses" ($1,085,760 in four seasons of racing, 1947–1951) **Sword Dancer** in the single racing year of 1959, won $537,004.

FAMOUS JOCKEYS—Eddie Arcaro has won the Kentucky Derby five times. **Isaac Murphy**, the great Negro jockey, and **Earl Sande**, each won the Derby three times. Arcaro is the only jockey to ride two Triple Crown winners (Whirlaway and Citation). England's **Sir Gordon Richards** is the only jockey ever knighted. **Johnie Longden** beat Sir Gordon's world record of 4,370 wins when he rode his 4,371st winner at Del Mar, California September 1, 1956. **Willie Shoemaker** became the first jockey to win $2,000,000 (in purses) in a single year (1956).

GOVERNING BODIES—Each **State Racing Commission** prescribes the rules, regulations and conditions of racing in that state. It issues licenses to owners, trainers and jockeys.

The Jockey Club is custodian of the American Thoroughbred Stud Book. (All North American-bred thoroughbreds may be recorded here.) The Jockey Club registers racing colors for New York and several other states and approves proposed names of horses. It established the pattern and code on which the State Racing Commissions' rules and regulations are based. The Jockey Club of England is a separate organization. The American Club is located at 300 Park Avenue, New York.

The Thoroughbred Racing Association is composed of the management of some 40 tracks throughout the country. It is concerned with matters of policy, the solution of mutual problems and the policing of tracks through its subsidiary, The Thoroughbred Racing Protective Bureau. Address: 405 Lexington Ave., New York.

THOROUGHBRED STUD BOOK—All horses included in the **American Thoroughbred Stud Book** are direct descents in the male line from one or more of the three foundation sires: the Darley Arabian, the Godolphin Barb and the Byerly Turk.

BAROMETER—The most effective barometer of the state of thorough-bred racing in the United States is generally considered to be the annual yearling sales at Saratoga, New York, and the Keeneland sales at Lexington, Kentucky—the number of yearlings offered for sale, the average price and the top prices.

THE SPORT—Harness racing is conducted with Standardbred **trotters** or **pacers** drawing a light, two-wheeled racing cart known as a **sulky**. A driver sits in the sulky and controls the horse through long reins. Many years ago, the racing cart was a high four-wheeled "wagon" —and then a large two-wheeled wagon with the driver sitting high. Prior to one hundred years ago, trotters were raced under saddle and trotting races under saddle are common in France and Belgium today.

Harness racing is very popular abroad, especially in France, Italy, Belgium, Sweden, Russia, Australia and New Zealand. It originated, however, in the United States.

THE SULKY—The sulky has small, bicycle-type wheels and the driver's seat is on a level with the shafts. The racing sulky weighs about 30 pounds and some are as light as 26 pounds. The term is said to derive from a sports-minded American wife, who seeing the single seat, contended that only a "sulky" man would want such a vehicle.

THE HORSE—The horses used in harness racing in the United States are a distinctive breed known since 1879 as the **American Standardbred**. They either trot or pace.

Messenger, a gray running horse stallion imported from England in 1788, is generally agreed to have provided the foundation stock for the Standardbred. However, the fastest harness horses today and for some time have included the great sire **Hambletonian** in their family tree. Hambletonian is, therefore, generally referred to as "Father of the Breed." **Mambrino Chief** and **Axworthy** were also dominant Standardbred sires.

As a rule, trotters and pacers do not race each other.

A **trotting** horse springs from one *diagonal* pair of legs to the other, e.g., the right fore and left hind—then the left fore and right hind.

A **pacing** horse springs from one *lateral* pair of legs to the other, e.g., the right fore and hind—then the left fore and hind.

137

THE PACE

The **pace** is a slightly faster gait than the **trot**, but only slightly so.

The age range of harness horses when they have established their best records is three to seven years old. Of course, some have been older, e.g., the famous **Flora Temple** at 14!

The length of a good trotter's stride is from 20 to 22 feet. **Greyhound's** stride was measured at 23 feet, **Titan Hanover's** at 22.

The greatest number of Standardbreds are bred in Ohio. Illinois is second, New York third. Indiana, Kentucky and Pennsylvania also breed large numbers of Standardbred horses. The largest Standardbred breeding establishments are in Kentucky and Pennsylvania. Hanover Shoe Farms in Pennsylvania and Walnut Hill Farm in Kentucky have produced more champions than all the others.

Factors affecting a harness horse's racing speed, in addition to the speed of the horse itself are: the driver, the sulky, shoeing, the track and the weather.

Horses whose natural gait is a trot can be taught to pace by use of hopples (leather straps looped about each pair of the horse's lateral legs) and horses whose natural gait is a pace may be trained to trot by the use of weighted shoes. However, the latter is seldom done since pacing is less natural and more difficult to maintain.

Harness horses frequently wear **quarter boots** (bell shaped, hinged and close fitting) as a protection against over-reaching.

Famous Standardbred Sires—The progenitors of famous Standardbred blood lines are **Messenger**, the foundation sire; **Hambletonian**, for whom the famous race is named; **Black Hawk, Justin Morgan, Bellfounder, Henry Clay, Mambrino Chief, Pilot Jr., Axworthy, Peter the Great** and **George Wilkes.**

Famous mares are **Lady Suffolk, Flora Temple, The Kent Mare, Nancy Hanks** and **Lou Dillon.**

Hambletonian traces his breeding on both sides to **Messenger** (the foundation sire) who was his great grandsire through both his sire, **Abdallah** and his dam, **The Kent Mare.**

138

THE TROT

U.S.T.A. TROTTING REGISTER—Eligibility for inclusion in the United States Trotting Association's **trotting register** is based on: (a) registered Standardbred sire or dam or (b) a registered Standardbred sire —dam and grand dam sired by a Standardbred horse; (c) a standard record; (d) being a sire or dam of two or more performers with standard records (there are four specific requirements under this general classification—one for stallions, three for mares), or (e) the approval of a specially appointed committee of breeders.

Originally, admission to the Trotting Register required only a recorded mile of 2:30 minutes trotting or 2:25 pacing. This was "standard," hence the name Standardbred.

CLASSIFICATION—In order to assure fair and interesting competition, racing Standardbreds are classified as to the time in which they can usually trot or pace a mile, e.g., 2:00 (a mile in 2 minutes—a very superior horse), 2:05, 2:10, etc. Horses are also classified as to the amount of their winnings. Races are usually limited to horses of specified time classifications.

A **classified** race is one open to horses named by a committee or a specially designated person (a classifier). The horses are selected because of their presumed ability to compete on an equal basis.

A **free for all** race is one not limited to time or money-winning classification—usually classic events in which, as a rule, only the fastest horses are entered.

A **bar** race is one limited to horses which have not won a race at a designated official time or less, e.g., a 2:05 bar trot is limited to horses which have not won a race timed in 2 minutes and 5 seconds or less.

THE GRAND CIRCUIT—The "Grand Circuit" is an association of harness race tracks and associations in the most important centers of harness racing with generally fixed purses and uniform conditions. The Grand

139

Circuit is, in some ways, comparable to the Big Leagues in baseball.

THE TRACK—Harness racing tracks are usually one-half mile or a mile and the horses trot or pace counterclockwise, the same direction as in Thoroughbred racing.

Races are usually one mile, although there are several two mile races at the bigger tracks.

Sometime ago, harness races were generally decided on the best two out of three **heats**. While a few of the classic races (The Hambletonian and The Little Brown Jug) and some at the small tracks are still raced in heats, this type of competition is rapidly vanishing and each race is now generally final.

The first trotting race held on a regular track was at Centerville, Long Island, New York on May 16th, 1826.

The greatest number of harness racing tracks in regular use is in Ohio. However, the greatest number of regular race meetings is in New York. Lexington, Ky., is usually considered to be the capital city of harness racing, while Orange County in New York is generally known as the birthplace of harness racing.

The largest purses and the greatest number of races are held at Roosevelt Raceway and the Yonkers Raceway, both near New York City.

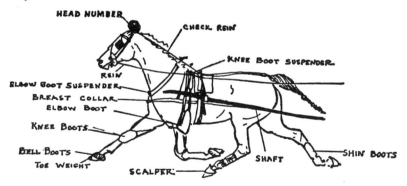

TERMS—**Scoring** refers to brief warm-up dashes prior to the start and, where there is no starting gate, to trotting or pacing in hand to the starting line.

Brushing refers to a short dash at top speed generally on approaching the finish. At one time, the term also described short informal races between two or more road drivers—popular on the highways and speedways up to the turn of the century.

Sidewheeler, sandshifter, and **wiggler**—All are slang phrases to describe a pacer.

Hopples are leather straps looped about each pair of a pacer's lateral legs to cause him to pace and to keep him from breaking.

Cheating refers to a horse sulking and not doing his best in a race.

A twice around is a ½ mile track.

Breaking—breaking the trot or pace by galloping—a serious fault.

Blowout—A leisurely workout, often on the day before a race.

Toe-weights—Two to six-ounce weights of brass or lead, attached to the front hoof to improve a horse's gait or lengthen his stride.

Double-header—A two-mile warm up, usually at a slow pace, on the afternoon of the race.

Fresh-legged—Applies to pacers which race without hopples.

Going big—Using up a horse's speed so that he has nothing left for a strong finish.

Jughead—Slang term for a horse addicted to stepping on his feet or making other mistakes in a race.

Pole—Starting position nearest to the inside rail of the track. When a handicapper gives the horses their positions, he frequently places the best horse on the far outside and gives the least qualified horse the favorable pole position.

Out on the limb—This means that a horse has "lapped on" to another horse at the rail and can't get in. Caught in this position, the horse usually tires and drops back.

FIXTURES AND RECORDS—The **most popular** and generally considered the most important harness race in the United States is the **Hambletonian Stake** for three year olds, raced for many years at Goshen, New York but, since 1957, at DuQuoin, Illinois.

Other **important races**, considered to be tops in their classification, are: the Horseman Stake at Indianapolis for two-year old trotters; the Fox Stake for two-year old pacers; the Little Brown Jug and Messenger Stakes for three-year old pacers and the Western Harness Racing Association's American Classic for older trotters and pacers.

The **trotting record** for a mile is 1:55¼ by **Greyhound** on September 29, 1938 at Lexington, Ky. (It is interesting that this famous horse, in addition to his color, was distinguished by his height, 16.1¼, and that he was an unprepossessing yearling, sold for $800.) He also won the Hambletonian in 1935.

The **pacing record** for a mile is 1.54⅗ by **Adios Butler** on October 4, 1960 at Lexington, Kentucky.

On the record, **male horses** have the better score. Since **Nancy Hanks'** 2:04 mile in 1892, seven out of nine new records have been established by stallions or geldings. In 21 Hambletonians, only seven fillies have won.

The time for a **fast mile** has changed considerably over the years: in 1870, it was about 2:20—the record was 2:17¼, in 1900, it was 2:05 —with a record of 2:03¼, in 1920, it was 2:00—the record was 1:58.

The first horses to trot or pace a **two minute mile** established their records not in a race, but directly against time behind a running horse and a shield to eliminate wind resistance.

The first **two minute** or better mile harness record was established August 28, 1897—the time was 1:59¼ by **Star Pointer**, a pacer at Reidville, Massachusetts—only four seconds slower than the present record.

Dan Patch paced in two minutes or faster, 30 times between 1901 and his retirement in 1909. His record, 1:55¼—set in 1905—stood for 33 years!

The mile was trotted in two minutes or better in 1903—the time, a flat 2:00—by **Lou Dillon** at Reidville, Massachusetts. In the same year, however, at Memphis, Tennessee, she trotted a mile in 1:58½— 3¼ seconds slower than the present record.

The long distance record against time is 20 miles in 58 minutes 21 seconds by **Blackrod**, driven by R. L. Parker, at Aiken, South Carolina in 1942.

THE GAME—Polo is played both outdoors and indoors.

Outdoors, the field is 300 yards long and 160 yards wide. The goal posts are 24 feet apart. Ten-inch high boards retain the ball on the playing field.

There are **four players** on a side: Number 1, Number 2, Number 3 and the Back.

The **ball** is made of willow root or similar hard wood. It is solid and covered with a heavy coat of glossy white paint. The ball weighs approximately 4½ ounces and is 3¼ inches in diameter. (About ¼ inch in diameter larger than a baseball and about ½ ounce lighter than a baseball.)

The ball is hit with the flat side of the mallet head. The **mallet** head is usually made of maple, sycamore, ash or elm and has a shaft of short jointed tapered cane or Malacca. It weighs about one pound and is about 50 inches long. A cotton tape thong, wound around the thumb, avoids losing the mallet.

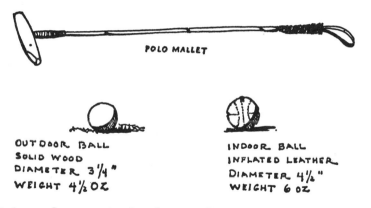

POLO MALLET

OUTDOOR BALL
SOLID WOOD
DIAMETER 3¼"
WEIGHT 4½ OZ

INDOOR BALL
INFLATED LEATHER
DIAMETER 4½"
WEIGHT 6 OZ

Indoors, the game is played in a riding arena and, therefore, the size varies considerably. Ideally, the indoor polo arena should be about 100 yards long by 50 wide. Instead of goal posts, the ball is hit against a marked (usually stripes painted on a wall) area on either end of the ring, 10 feet wide. The arena may be enclosed by knee-boards about 3½ feet high. The footing is usually tanbark, shavings or dirt or a mixture of these.

The **ball** is inflated—a leather cover with a rubber bladder—about 1½ times as large as the outdoor ball. It looks like a miniature soccer or basketball and is white. Since it is light (6–6½ oz.) it "floats" on the uneven footing, where the much heavier and smaller outdoor ball would be lost in it. Since it is lighter, the same stroke will not cause it to travel as far as the wooden outdoor ball and, because of the close quarters, use of the inflated ball is less dangerous to horses, players and spectators.

The **mallet** is the same as that used outdoors. There are **three players** on a side instead of four—Number 1, Number 2 and the Back.

Both indoor and outdoor polo games are divided into a number of **periods**, usually six outdoors and four indoors. These periods are 7½ minutes each and are frequently referred to as "chukkers" or "chukkas" (an East Indian term).

A mounted referee officiates. He throws in the ball when it goes out of bounds or after a goal is scored, calls fouls, and awards penalties for these fouls. In important "cup" or championship matches outdoors, there are sometimes two mounted referees and a dismounted umpire.

CLOTHING AND TACK—All players are required to wear a protective cap. Distinctive "jerseys" or shirts with the number of the wearer's position, white breeches, brown boots and spurs compose the usual polo uniform. Spurs must not be pointed or contain rowels.

The tack used by polo players on their mounts consists usually of a Pelham bridle, a standing martingale and a deep seated flat (English) saddle. The polo pony's legs are usually protected by felt "boots," or bandages. Ponies' tails are usually braided and wrapped to minimize interference with the swing of the mallet.

POLO PONIES—The mount used for polo is commonly referred to as a "pony." However, it is not technically a pony, but rather a small horse. Prior to 1915, the height of polo mounts was limited to 14.2 hands so that they were properly ponies. In 1915, the limit was placed at 15.1 and, since 1920, there has been no limitation as to height. Nowadays, polo mounts are usually from 15 to 15.2 hands in height and usually weigh from 850 to 1150 lbs. These small horses are sometimes Thoroughbreds, but more often ¾ or ½ Thoroughbred.

The most desirable **characteristics** are speed; handiness (ability to turn sharply and quickly, stop promptly and go on again quickly); stamina and endurance; and a willingness to "ride off" an opponent. The polo mount must also, of course, be used to the swinging mallet and not shy of the ball.

There is a general misconception that a polo pony follows the ball. This is not true. The polo pony is very sensitive to its rider's aids (reins and legs) and particularly his change of balance and, therefore, he *seems* naturally to follow the ball. Often his rider does *not* want him to follow the ball.

Polo ponies generally begin tournament play at six years of age and frequently at seven. Occasionally, but not desirably, they begin at five.

Polo ponies' shoes are light and usually made from rim steel bars. The front shoes have no calks; the hind shoes are calked.

THE RULES—A goal counts 1 point.

Fouls are penalized by a variety of free shots for the goal, with or without a defender. Most common fouls are: crossing a player who has the right of way so close that it might cause a collision or be dangerous; pulling across the line the ball is travelling so as to endanger oneself or the player who has the right of way; not giving way to the player who has the right of way when riding from a different direction, and not giving way to two players approaching from the opposite direction; dangerous riding; zigzagging in front of another player at a gallop; stopping or pulling up on the ball; unduly rough play; etc.; dangerous and illegal use of the mallet such as hooking an opponent's mallet across his pony's forelegs or across the back of his mount.

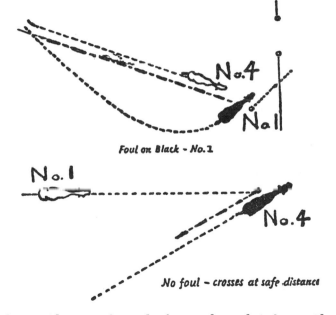

Foul on Black - No. 1

No foul - crosses at safe distance

Outdoors, sides are changed after each goal—**indoors** sides are changed only at the end of each period.

A tie at the end of a game is usually broken by a "sudden death" period of five minutes. The team first scoring a goal in this sudden death period wins the match.

HANDICAPS—Players are handicapped **zero** to **ten**. Zero players are the least experienced—ten-goal players the most experienced and

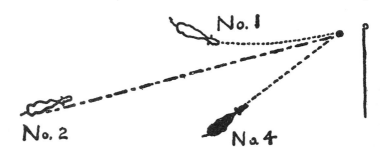

capable. In any year, there are few ten-goal players; a good half of the some 200 players listed by the United States Polo Association are rated zero; one to four-goal players are the next larger group and only about 10% are rated in excess of four goals. Handicaps of individual players are added together to determine a team handicap. In match play, the team with the lower handicap starts with a score equal to the difference between its team handicap and the opponents' team handicap.

The United States Polo Association lists a handful of "greats"—the **ten-goal players:**

R. L. Agassiz	Michael G. Phipps
Elmer J. Bostwick, Jr.	Robert Skene
J. E. Cowden	Cecil Smith
Thomas Hitchcock, Sr.	Malcolm Stevenson
Thomas Hitchcock, Jr.	L. E. Stoddard
Stewart B. Iglehart	J. M. Waterbury
Foxhall Keene	L. Waterbury
Devereux Milburn	J. Watson Webb
	H. P. Whitney

HISTORY—The game of polo is generally believed to have originated in Persia. Written records and drawings indicate that a contest between mounted men and women, each equipped with a mallet for stroking a ball through goal posts, known apparently as "chaugan" was popular at the Persian court as early as 590 A.D. Records also indicate that the game was known to the ancient Greeks and the Chinese as well as the Persians before the Christian era. The game was common in India before the 16th century. Japan still plays its form of polo, called Dakiu, introduced there from Tibet and China over 400

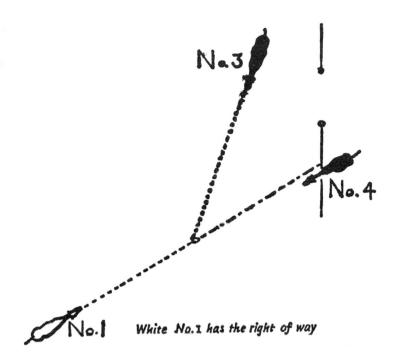

White No. 1 has the right of way

years ago. Polo was first played in England in 1869 by the 10th Hussars and was adopted by the Hurlingham Club in 1873.

The word "polo" appears to be an adaptation of the Tibetan word "Pulu" meaning a ball. Polo was introduced to the United States by James Gordon Bennett, the famous publisher, in 1876 in New York City, indoors in Dickel's Riding Academy at Fifth Avenue and 39th Street. Not long after, it was played outdoors at the Polo Grounds in upper Manhattan, New York City—later the home baseball grounds of the New York Giants.

The famous Westchester ("National") Cup for competition between England and the United States was first played for at Newport, Rhode Island in August 1886. It was named after the first polo club in the United States—the Westchester Club of New York City and Newport, Rhode Island. The United States was consistently successful in winning the matches for this trophy, taking nine out of twelve.

Most famous sires of polo stock were **Prince Friarstown** and **Christopher Columbus.**

ROUND ROBIN—A Round Robin is a polo match in which three teams compete in pairs on the same field in one event. Generally, there are three matches of two or three periods each, e.g., Team A plays

Team B for two periods; then Team A plays Team C for two periods; then B plays C for two periods. The winner is the team which has the best record of matches won or tied—or, in the event of an all around tie, the one having the greatest number of net goals to its credit.

PADDOCK POLO—This is, in effect, indoor polo played on an unfinished outdoor field or paddock—three on a side and using an inflated ball, except that there are goal posts instead of the backboard.

GOVERNING BODY—The governing body of polo in the United States is the **United States Polo Association**. It prescribes the rules and regulations of play and handicaps players. The Association sponsors and conducts annual championship tournaments in various handicap classes and an "open" championship. Its headquarters is at 250 Park Ave., New York.

A **Gymkhana** is a meeting of horsemen and horsewomen of all ages to engage in informal mounted games. These are particularly suitable for children and inexperienced riders, for boy and girl scout troops, for pony clubs and for summer camps as a means of improving ability, providing variation and increasing interest in their riding. Some of the mounted games usually included in a Gymkhana are:

MUSICAL CHAIRS—Played in the same manner as if the contestants were not mounted. One less chair than the number of riders; at a whistle, gong or cessation of music, they dismount and make for one of the chairs holding on to the reins. The one without a chair drops out and a chair is removed, etc.

EGG AND SPOON RACE—The first rider to finish with the egg in a spoon, carried in one hand, is the winner. The distance traversed may vary—125 yards is a good one. The contest may be conducted at a walk, trot or canter.

WATER RACE—Contestants, with a glass in the hand at the starting point, dismount, fill their glasses ¾ or more full from a pail (usually one for each rider or each two riders), mount and race about 25 yards. The first one to cross the finish line with the glass not less than half full wins. If desired, the contestants may start mounted with their glasses nearly full.

Another variation is to dismount and drink the water remaining in the glass—provided it is at least half full. A further variation is to carry a full glass on a small tray from the start to the finish

BUN EATING CONTEST—The contestants race from a start to a designated other line, dismount, eat a bun, mount and return to the start. Of course, the first one to return to the starting line wins.

GRETNA GREEN RACE—Men or boys race from a starting line a distance of 50 yards, pick up a woman or girl and return to the starting line with their "brides" in the saddle with them. The first couple in wins.

POLO BALL STROKING CONTEST—Each contestant is given a polo mallet and polo ball painted a different color. (For this reason, if there is a large number, the contest must be conducted in heats.) The object is to hit the ball across a line about 100 to 150 yards away (150 is better). Any contestant may stroke any other contestant's ball out of that contestant's way to spoil his progress. There are, therefore, two objectives—to stroke your own ball over the goal line first and stroke to the side or backwards any nearby other contestant's.

SADDLING AND BRIDLING RACE—The contestants line up on a starting line, bridles and saddles on that line, holding their mount with a halter and halter shank. At a signal, the contestants bridle and saddle their horses, mount carrying their halters, race to the finish line, unsaddle, unbridle and halter their horses. The saddle and bridle must be on the ground in an orderly and appropriate manner. The first to accomplish this is the winner.

REMOVING THE SADDLE—This is a difficult contest, for advanced riders. The contestants race from a starting line to a designated other line, say 100 yards distant, and return to the starting line. While travelling this distance, they must remove the saddle while mounted and return to the starting line riding bareback and carrying the saddle. The first one in wins.

RELAY RACE—The contestants race from a starting line to a designated other line, say 100 yards distant, dismount and turn their mount over to a teammate who mounts and returns to the start. There may be anywhere from two to four or even more relays. The contest may be conducted with mounts saddled or bareback.

BALLOON SCRIMMAGE—Each contestant carries a balloon on a two-foot string—or, alternately, has one tied to his or her back or neck. The object of the contest is to burst the other contestants' balloons while keeping one's own intact. The last contestant to have his or her balloon intact is the winner. Pointed objects to burst the balloons are not permitted.

BAREBACK RACE—Contestants, mounted in saddles, race to a designated line. At this point, each contestant dismounts, removes his saddle, vaults onto his horse's back and races back to the starting line. The first one in is the winner.

GYMKHANA EVENTS FOR TEAMS OF FOUR—TEAM RELAY BENDING RACE—A team competition which may be run in heats if there are more than 6 teams.

Lines of five or six poles will be erected from 24 feet to 30 feet apart. The start and finish will be the same line, marked by flags at one end of the arena.

Number Ones of teams will pass down, and back, bending through the poles. Number Ones will then hand over batons to Number Twos. The "hand-over" must take place behind the starting line.

Number Twos will hand over to Number Threes, and Number Threes to Number Fours.

The winning team will be that team whose Number Four rider passes the finish line first.

Should the baton be dropped by either competitor during the "hand-over," the next competitor to go must dismount, and pick up the baton. Should a rider drop the baton during the time he is passing down the bending course, the rider will dismount, pick it up, mount and complete the course.

The following faults will incur elimination of the team from this event:

(a) Missing out a bending pole.
(b) Knocking a pole to the ground or breaking it.
(c) If the baton is dropped during the "hand-over," failure of the next rider to dismount and pick it up.
(d) Crossing the starting line before receiving the baton.

MUSICAL HATS—A team competition, all riders competing together.

A number of hats on posts will be placed in the center of the arena, the number being less by one or two than the number of riders competing. Posts will be erected in a circle around the hats.

The riders will follow around on the outside of the circle. When the band stops or a whistle is blown, the riders will gallop to the center, dismount and put on the hats, remaining dismounted.

One or two hats will be removed each time until only one rider is left in.

Points will be awarded for individual placings as follows: The rider or riders eliminated in the first round score, 1 point each. Those eliminated in the second round, 2 points, and so on. The last rider left in will score one point more than the rider eliminated in the last round.

Points of all four members of each team will be totalled and the winning team will be the one with the greatest number of points.

ANTI-LITTER CAMPAIGN—A team competition which may be run in heats if there are more than 8 teams.

Litter in the form of tins, boxes, or plastic-ware will be scattered in the center of the arena.

A container for each team will be placed at equal distances from the center.

The first pair from each team will start at their respective containers, the second pair remaining outside the arena. Each rider will be armed with a stick or bamboo cane from 3 to 4 feet in length.

On the word "Go" the riders will gallop to the center, pick up a piece of litter on the end of the stick and return to dump it in the container. They will continue to collect litter in this way until it is all collected (or until a whistle is blown after a set period of 1 to 1½ minutes).

The first pairs will withdraw and the amount of litter they have dumped into their container will be counted. The litter will then be rescattered into the center of the arena if necessary.

155

The second pairs will then go to their respective containers ready to start.

On the word "Go" the second pairs will collect litter in the same way until it is all collected (or until the whistle is blown after a set period of 1 to 1½ minutes).

The litter collected by the second pairs will be counted and the team whose two pairs have collected the greatest amount of litter will be the winner.

The riders must remain mounted and must not touch the litter by hand when picking it up, carrying it on the stick and dumping it.

Should any litter fall off the stick or fail to drop into the container when dumped in, the rider may either pick it up again on his stick or leave it where it is and go on to collect another piece.

No litter may be dumped after the whistle is blown.

If a container is knocked over, a rider must dismount, replace the container and put all the litter back into it by hand. He may continue to do this after the whistle has blown and all will be counted.

LED PONY RACE—A team competition which may be run in heats if there are more than 6 teams.

Four poles or wooden horses will be erected as for a bending race, at about 24 to 30 feet apart. Flags will be placed to mark the start or finish at each end of the arena.

Number Ones will form up mounted, leading Number Twos' mounts, Number Threes will form up behind the Number Ones dismounted and holding Number Fours' mounts. Number Twos and Number Fours will form up at the far end of the arena, Number Two holding Number Three's mount.

On the word "Go" Number One will ride down the course, through the bending poles, leading Number Two's mount. On reaching Number Two, he will hand over Number Two's mount to him. Number Two will then mount and pass down the line of posts, taking Number Three's mount with him.

Number One will hand over his mount to Number Four after Number Two has started. Number Two, on reaching Number Three, will hand him his mount, and Number Three will then pass down the line of posts, handing over Number Four's mount to Number Four. Number Four will pass down the course, leading Number One's mount. The winning team will be that whose Number Four rider crosses the finish line first leading Number One's pony.

Mounting must be done behind the flags marking the start and finish at either end of the course.

Should a rider and led mount fail to pass the correct side of a post, or knock one down, or break one, their team will be eliminated.

Only the rider handing over a pony may help the next rider.

SHIRT RACE—A team competition which may be run in heats if there are more than 6 teams.

Starting and finishing lines will be marked by flags at both ends of the arena. A center line will also be marked halfway between the start and finish lines.

Number Ones and Threes will be mounted at one end of the arena, and Number Twos and Fours at the other end. Number Ones will each carry a shirt.

On the word "Go" Number Ones will gallop forward, dismount and get into their shirts, mount again before crossing the center line, gallop on to the end of the arena, dismount, remove their shirts and hand them to their Number Twos.

Number Twos, Threes and Fours will complete the course in the same way up and down the arena successively.

Removing the shirt and handing it over must be done behind the finishing line.

The winning team will be the one whose Number Four crosses the finishing line first in his shirt, mounted.

POTATO PICKING SCRAMBLE—A team competition with up to 6 teams taking part together.

A sack of potatoes is emptied and spread out in small piles in the center of the arena. A basket, or bucket, for each team will be placed at equal distances from the center.

One member of each team will start at their respective buckets, the second remains outside the arena.

On the word "Go" the riders in the arena will gallop to the center, dismount, pick up a potato, mount and return to their buckets, drop the potato into the bucket and return for another.

At the conclusion of a minute, a whistle will be blown. On this signal, the first riders of each team will immediately withdraw and the second riders of each team will go to their buckets to get ready to start.

On the word "Go" the second riders of each team will collect potatoes and drop them into their buckets for 1 minute. The whistle will then be blown again, and the second rider will withdraw.

The rider must be mounted when dropping the potato into the bucket, but should he miss the bucket or should the potato bounce out, the rider must dismount, pick up the potato, mount and drop the potato into the bucket. No potato may be dropped into a bucket after the whistle has blown.

Should the bucket be knocked over, a rider must dismount, replace the bucket and put all the potatoes into it again. He may continue to do this after the whistle has blown (but no additional potatoes may be put in) and all will be counted.

If all of the potatoes in the arena have been placed in buckets before the fourth riders have gone, additional potatoes are placed in the arena.

SADDLE RELAY RACE—A team competition which may be run in heats if there are more than 6 teams.

There will be a start and finishing line at each end of the arena.

Lines of four posts as for Bending will be placed about 24 feet apart.

Each team will be allowed one saddle. Stirrups and leathers are optional. Girths must have two buckles.

Number Ones and Threes will wait at one end of the arena. Number Twos and Fours will wait at the opposite end, all dismounted and holding their mounts behind the starting lines. The saddles will be placed on the ground in a line halfway between the start and the finish posts.

On the word "Go" the Number Ones will lead their mounts to the saddles, saddle up, mount and pass to the end of the arena through the bending posts. On reaching the opposite end the Number Ones will dismount and hand the saddle behind the finishing line to the Number Twos who will saddle up and mount. Number Twos will then pass down course to Number Threes where they will change over in the same way. Number Threes will then pass to Number Fours who will finish the course.

The winning team will be the one whose Number Four is the first to pass the finishing line mounted.

The rider handing over may assist the next rider to saddle and mount.

The riders must remain mounted on the course. If a rider falls off after he has started on the course he must remount, but he need not replace the saddle if it has come off. He may carry it instead.

BALLOON RACE—A team competition which may be run in heats if there are more than 6 teams.

The start and finish will be the same line at one end of the arena.

A number of inflated balloons are attached to a pole for each team, at the other end of the arena.

The Number One of each team will gallop to the balloons, collect one from his team's pole, and return to the starting line.

The balloon will then be handed to the Number Two who will gallop carrying it back to the pole of balloons, and collect a second balloon, returning with these two to the Number Three who will collect the third balloon, handing over to the Number Four who will collect the fourth.

The winning team will be that team whose fourth rider is first past the finish line mounted with four balloons.

The "hand-over" must be done behind the starting line.

Should a balloon burst, or float away, the rider must return and collect another.

Should a balloon be dropped during the "hand-over," the rider next to go must dismount, pick up the balloon, remount, and continue. Should a rider during his turn drop a balloon, he must dismount, and pick it up again.

EGG AND SPOON RACE—A team competition which may be run in heats if there are more than 6 teams.

Lines of three posts will be placed as for the Bending Race. On the center post of each line will be fixed a container in which will be placed spare eggs. The starting and finishing line will be marked by flags at one end of the arena.

Teams will line up mounted behind the starting line. Number Ones will each carry a spoon on which is placed an egg.

At the word "Go" the Number Ones will ride up and down the line through the bending posts carrying their eggs on their spoons. The eggs must not be touched by hand.

On arrival at the finishing line, Number Ones will hand their spoons and eggs to their Number Twos, the eggs still untouched by hand. Numbers Twos, Threes and Fours will complete the course in the same way up and down the arena successively.

The winning team will be the one whose Number Four crosses the finishing line first carrying his egg on his spoon.

Should the egg be dropped, the rider must collect another one from the container on his team's center post and resume the course again from the point where he dropped the egg. The egg need not be placed on the spoon until this point is reached. Should a rider drop his spoon and egg, he must dismount, pick them both up, remount, place the egg on the spoon and continue the course.

Should the spoon and/or egg be dropped, during the "hand-over," the rider next to go must take the appropriate action.

THE ALERT—A team competition which may be run in heats if there are more than 6 teams.

Teams are formed up in the center of the arena. Riders dismount and unsaddle their mounts. All four saddles are placed in line behind the mounts, which are held by one member of each team.

The three remaining riders of each team remove their hats, which are mixed up and spread over a fairly wide area. While facing away from the arena, the three riders stand behind the starting line.

A whistle is blown and the alert is sounded. The three riders collect their hats, put them on, and then with the fourth rider saddle the mounts, mount up and complete the course together.

The winning team will be the one first past the finish line.

Hats may be marked on the inside only.

The teams are inspected at the finish and if a girth buckle is undone or a rider is not wearing his own hat, the team is eliminated.

May be contested with or without stirrups.

VEGETABLE RACE—A team competition which may be run in heats if there are more than 6 teams.

The start and finish will be the same line at one end of arena. Lines of two, three or four posts will be erected as for a Bending Race. These posts will each have a container fixed firmly to it at about 4 feet from the ground. In each container will be placed an apple, a carrot, an orange, and a potato. A bucket or basket will be placed 15 feet in front of the starting line opposite each line of posts.

Each Number One will collect an apple and return with it, dropping it into the bucket. The rider will then return and collect a second apple, and so on, until all the apples are collected.

As soon as the last apple is in the bucket and the Number One has crossed the finishing line mounted, Number Two will commence collecting carrots, and the Number Three collecting oranges and the Number Four collecting potatoes.

The winning team will be the one whose fourth rider first crosses the finish line mounted after having collected all his potatoes.

Should an apple, carrot, orange or potato be dropped outside the bucket or bounce out the rider must dismount, pick it up, mount and drop it into the bucket. Should the bucket be knocked over the rider must dismount, replace all the articles in the bucket, mount and continue. Should a rider collect and drop a wrong article into the bucket his team will be eliminated.

SHARPSHOOTERS RACE—A team competition which may be run in heats if there are more than 6 teams.

The start and finish will be at one end of the arena. At the other end will be a row of ten pins on boxes—three for each team.

Number One and Three are mounted bareback behind the start. Number Two and Four stand at the heads of Number One and Three's mounts.

At the word "Go" Number Two and Four will mount on to Number One and Three's mounts and the two pairs will then gallop to the center line. Number Two and Four will dismount before crossing the center line, and run to a line of buckets containing baseballs or tennis balls, about 15 feet in front of the ten pins. Number Two and Four will throw the balls at the ten pins until they are knocked down. They run back to the mounts, remount before crossing the center line and gallop to the finish.

The winning team is the one which has both pairs of riders first over the finish line mounted.

Number One and Three remain mounted but, should a rider fall off, he must remount at the same place and continue the course.

FLAG RACE—A team competition which may be run in heats if there are more than 6 teams.

There will be a start and finish line at each end of the arena. Four flag holders (upturned drain pipes or oil drums) for each team will be put up in the same positions as bending poles. A white flag will be placed in the first holder of each team, green in the second, red in the third and yellow in the fourth. All flags will be on poles 3 to 4 feet long. Numbers One and Three will be at one end of the arena and Numbers Two and Four at the other. Number One will carry a blue flag.

On the word "Go" Number One will gallop to the first holder, place the blue flag in it and remove the white one. He will carry the white flag to the second holder, place the flag in it and remove the green one. He will carry the green flag to the third holder, place the flag in it and remove the red one. He will carry the red flag to the fourth holder, place the flag in it and remove the yellow one. He will carry the yellow flag and hand it on to Number Two.

Number Two will then gallop to the nearest holder (where Number One had left the red flag). Number Two will put the yellow flag into this holder and remove the red flag. He will carry the red flag to the next holder and so change the flags in succession back to their original positions until he hands the blue flag on to Number Three.

Number Three will change over the flags in succession in a similar manner to Number One and he will hand the yellow flag on to Number Four. Number Four will then return all the flags back to their original positions in succession and will carry the blue flag over the finish.

The winning team will be the one whose Number Four is first over the finish line carrying the blue flag.

Should a flag be dropped the rider must dismount and pick it up. At a "hand-over" the next to go must pick it up. The "hand-over" must be done behind the start or finish line.

Should a flag holder be knocked over, the rider must dismount and set it up again.

If flags are placed improperly, this must be corrected by the rider on the course. (i.e. the one who placed them incorrectly.)

MOUNTED WRESTLING—Teams are eight or more on a side, bareback or with a blanket and surcingle. Each side advances from a different end of the field. The idea is to unseat the opponent while remaining mounted oneself. If any part of the body touches the ground, it is considered equivalent to being unseated and contestant must withdraw. The side which has one or more members still up after all the others have been unseated wins.

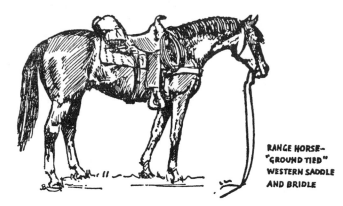

RANGE HORSE—
"GROUND TIED"
WESTERN SADDLE
AND BRIDLE

THE RANGE HORSE—The **typical range horse** or "cow pony" used in working cattle is of unknown ancestry, but is obviously descended from the horses brought over by the Spanish Conquistadores. They tend to be on the small side, about 15 hands—ranging from 14 to 16 —somewhat smaller in the southwest than in the northwest. They are handy (able to stop and turn quickly, to change direction on the correct lead and to respond promptly to neck reins), surefooted, rugged, courageous, and they subsist well on the limited forage and water found on the Western plains.

Most of the horses bred in the West for market are **Thoroughbreds** and **Thoroughbred Types** with varying infusions of Thoroughbred and Quarter Horse blood. They are bred for sale to interests which plan to use them for flat racing, polo, hunting and police work—and to parade organizations, cavalry units, etc.

The greatest **number of range horses** are bred and raised in Texas. California, Wyoming and Colorado are next.

The greatest number of and largest horse **ranches** are in Texas and California.

The **Quarter Horse** is a registered breed of western U. S. horse much used for working stock, for rodeos and on ranches. It is characterized by a notable burst of speed at short distances—about a quarter mile. Thus, the name. The Quarter Horse is relatively short, "built low to the ground," with thick short cannons, well muscled and stocky. He is a "good keeper." The breed originated in Virginia in the 1760's. Today's Quarter Horse appears to be largely a product of Thoroughbred sires and Spanish Mustang dams.

Range horses are frequently **branded** on the near flank, shoulder or neck with the ranch's distinctive mark.

RANGE CATTLE—The most usual type of beef cattle raised on the Western plains today is the **Hereford** or **"white face."** The breed of cattle known as **Santa Gertrudis**—a cross between the Indian Brahma and the Shorthorn—popularized by the King Ranch, is found in increasing numbers today as is also the **Aberdeen Angus.**

LONGHORN

Many years ago, the **"longhorn"** predominated in the Western range. This was a long horned variety of only fair beef cattle which migrated north from Old Mexico; it is now almost extinct. It has been replaced by the **shorthorn.**

A **steer** is a castrated male of one of the cattle breeds.

The greatest **number of beef cattle** are raised in Texas. The next largest number in Iowa. Large numbers of cattle are also raised in Kansas, Nebraska, Minnesota and Colorado.

The cattle in the Northern plains stat s, like the horses, are somewhat larger and heavier than they are in the South.

The greatest number of and largest cattle **ranches** are in Texas, Colorado, Kansas and Florida.

Cattle are generally **branded.**

COUGAR

OTHER PLAINS ANIMALS—In addition to beef cattle and horses, a large number of **sheep** are ranged on the Western plains.

As a carryover from the days of the open range, sheep ranchers are unpopular with the horse and cattle ranchers since the sheep nibble the grass so short as to make it entirely useless for grazing cattle and horses, and because their small sharp hoofs cut the grass into the ground and kill it. Since there is now little open range, there seems no need for any feuding between the two groups. In the mountainous country bordering the Southwest plains, **mountain lions** or **cougars** are disturbingly plentiful. These predatory animals are a great danger to horses and cattle as are coyotes on the plains.

SLANG—**Arroyo**—A dried-up stream bed; a gully. (From the Spanish.)

Broke horse—One that is sufficiently manageable to bridle, saddle and ride with reasonable safety.

Broomtail—A wild horse, usually small, slight and not worth the bother of "breaking" or training.

Bronc—An unbroken or untamed horse, or a horse that, although it has been broken and ridden, remains intractable, mean, dangerous and untrustworthy. The term is also sometimes used to describe the Western "cow pony" whether broken or unbroken and without regard to its "orneriness." The term comes from the Spanish "bronco" meaning wild or untamed.

Buckaroo—A hard riding cowhand whose chief occupation is breaking broncs. Sometimes also applied to rodeo riders. (Probably a corruption of the Spanish "vaquero.")

Cayuse—An Indian pony.

CHUCK WAGON

Chuck wagon—A horse-drawn commissary and supply wagon in which food, cooking untensils, fuel and a crude stove are carried to furnish meals.

Critter—A calf. The term is, however, frequently applied to range cattle generally.

Cutting out calves—Using a cow pony to separate a special group of calves from the herd by "hazing" them into a position to be roped by another man on a rope pony and taken out of the herd. The term is usually applied to the operation of separating unbranded calves preparatory to branding. (This is now usually accomplished in a corral.)

Dogie—Originally, a motherless calf, but now frequently applied to young scrub cattle of poor quality.

Dude—Anyone not a native of the West; originally one who dressed in a fashion not customary on the range and who was strange to the ways and customs of the range. Now frequently used to describe a paying guest at a western ranch.

Ground tie—Letting a horse's separated reins fall to the ground, hanging from the bit. The horse should stand quietly (tied to the ground) while the rider walks away.

Maverick—An unbranded calf, especially a motherless calf. Named for Samuel A. Maverick of Texas, who did not brand his calves.

Outlaw—A vicious horse that cannot be ridden with safety, and which regularly or periodically devotes its energies to unseating or disposing of its rider.

Pinto (or **paint**)—A piebald or skewbald horse (one with a mottled coat of dark hair marked with large spots or splotches of white.) Frequently they are also white faced.

Remuda—A collection of "broken" horses in a corral—or assembled on the plain—from which the horses to be ridden for the day's work are selected.

Riding herd—Riding slowly around a herd of cattle or horses to prevent any of the animals straying from it, to drive back stragglers and to prevent a stampede—controlling the herd.

Roundup—A periodic collection of all of a rancher's horses or cattle to take inventory of the stock, to brand young horses and calves and select stock for shipment to market.

Rustler—A cattle or horse thief.

Vaquero—The Mexican name for "Cow Boy."

Wrangler—A hand whose duty it is to watch and periodically assemble the "remuda" of horses for the others engaged in work on the plains.

FENCES—The fences found on the Western plains are almost entirely barbed wire. A length of fence is studded by gates. Also, in a length of fence, several of the posts are not driven into the ground so that a section of it may be turned and laid flat.

Since range horses are not as a rule jumped, cowhands get their horses on the other side of a wire fence—when they are not near a gate—by "laying" a section of the fence and leading the horses over it. (The horses are, of course, used to this.)

168

Cattlemen will tell you that if you are lost on the plains, the thing to do is to ride to a fence and follow it into a corral. This is good advice, providing you can find a fence!

TACK—The **stock** or **Western saddle** used by the Western cattlemen is distinguished by a high cantle and pommel, with a rather narrow space between them, a horn on the pommel to which a rope may be secured, and stirrups hung somewhat further back than they are on the **English** type saddle.

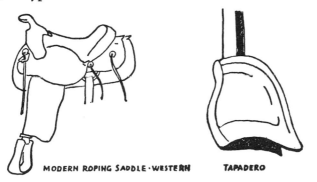

MODERN ROPING SADDLE · WESTERN   TAPADERO

The typical **bridle** is somewhat more simple than that used in "Eastern" riding. There is only a bit (rather than a bit and bridoon or Pelham bit) and there is no separate cavesson. Frequently too, there is no throat latch, the bridle being held in place by a slit in the headstall through which the near ear is passed.

A **bosal** is a cavesson noseband made of braided rawhide or leather.

The cowhand's bridle **reins** (one on each side) are *not* fastened together. This is so that, if the rider dismounts or is thrown, the reins will fall with the loose ends lying on the ground. Then, if the horse attempts to move away, it will step on the loose ends of the reins, apply pressure on the bit and stop itself. However, older horses, if they really wish to get away, have learned that they can do pretty well by turning their heads sideways and trailing the reins so that they do not step on them.

The **girth** or **cinch** is usually of the "string" variety. There are generally two girths, one for the forward and one for the rear part of the saddle. However, the "center fire rig" single girth—midway between the pommel and cantle—is also frequently used (in the Northwest largely).

A **latigo** is a cinchstrap used to draw the cinch tight through a ring on the saddle and a ring on the girth (cinch).

A **fender** is an oblong piece of wide leather attached to the stirrup leather of the stock saddle and is used to protect the rider's leg. The stirrups are frequently covered by a leather hood called a **tapadero.**

A **romal** is a round braid of rawhide (or horsehair) attached to the end of closed reins—and used as a **quirt** (a short handled whip of rawhide).

HOBBLE—A **hobble** is frequently used for fastening together a horse's forelegs to fetter him. It is usually composed of two straps which are buckled, one on each leg, just above the fetlock, and fastened together by a short strap or chain—or leather cuffs fastened by a chain. Sometimes the hobble is merely a rawhide tie and, occasionally, as a makeshift, a short length of rope is used.

SEAT—The cowboy's seat differs materially from that used in hunting and polo and, less, from that used by saddle horse people. The Western seat is distinguished by the long stirrups which cause the entire body to be nearly vertical, giving the effect of standing on the stirrups with the support of the cantle.

CLOTHES—The distinctive and well-known costume of the plains cattlemen is not bizarre—it serves a very useful purpose.

The broad brimmed **hat** is a protection against rain, hail and sun; the high crown provides an air space for coolness. It is called a **Stetson.**

The leather or fur **chaps** (the correct name is *chaparajos*—pronounced cha par áh hos) are worn to protect the legs from thorny or heavy brush, bumps against cattle or other horses and against severe weather.

The colorful bandanna **neckerchief** is lifted over the nose and mouth as a protection against the dust and, in the North, to tie over the ears in winter.

The high heels on the Westerner's **boots** prevent the foot slipping through the stirrup with the danger of being "hung up" if unseated or in the event of a fall, and to provide a secure hold and firm footing on the ground (by digging the heels in when roping from the ground).

The short height of the cowboy's boots makes them easy to put on and take off. It is a common practice in the Southwest, before putting on one's boots, to turn them upside down and tap the soles vigorously to rid them of tarantula, lizard, snake or other objectionable creature that may have crawled in.

The blue denim "jeans"—rather tight legged with riveted seam points—usually worn by stock men at work, are called **levis** because, for a long time, the most popular of these garments was made by Levi Straus of San Francisco.

Shotgun chaps are unadorned plain chaps, closed and fitting tightly over the leg like trousers. They are used frequently by rodeo and show riders as well as hands on ranches. They are characteristic of California.

Chinks are deerhide or buckskin (generally) abbreviated chaps something like a leather apron fastened to the legs—a sort of divided leather skirt worn by women in lieu of regular chaps.

The stockman's large roweled **spurs** are necessitated by the little time available for schooling horses, the necessity for prompt action and the independence of the range horse.

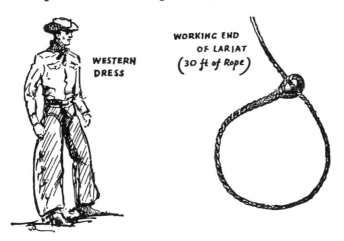

WESTERN DRESS

WORKING END
OF LARIAT
(30 ft of Rope)

LARIATS—The **lariat** (from the Spanish *la reata,* a rope) is a rope of small diameter with a running noose carried on the cowhand's saddle and used for catching or securing cattle or horses. It is frequently referred to also as a **lasso** and a **riata**. "Riata" is sometimes used to designate a rawhide rope as opposed to a grass "rope" or "lariat."

Usual length of the lariat is from 35 to 50 feet and, most commonly, it is from ⅜ to ½ inch in diameter. It is almost universally made of hemp. Infrequently now, it is made of braided rawhide, although in the earlier days, this was common. Cotton and nylon mixture lariats are also sometimes used today.

The metal eye which fits into the loop at the end of the lariat—through which the other end is passed to form a running noose—is called a **honda**.

RODEO—A **Rodeo** is an organized series of contests, public demonstrations and spectacles of the Western plains—with Western riding, riders, horses and cattle.

CUTTING HORSE *and* HEREFORD

Rodeo is **Spanish** for "roundup" (of cattle) and is pronounced either rō′ dē.ō or rō.dā′ō. The latter is usual in the Southwest.

The rodeo **originated** in the days of the unfenced ranges in the '70's. A kind of country fair was held following the semi-annual roundups, at which the cowhands of the several ranches, after they were paid off, incidentally entertained themselves with feats of skill and informal contests in connection with their work, as well as poker and the droning of ballads. These affairs gradually developed into local shows or exhibitions. The first well-organized, well-advertised rodeo was held in Denver in 1896.

A **chute** is a narrow wooden boxlike enclosure in which horses (so that they may be saddled and mounted) and cattle are placed awaiting their turns and from which they are released to take part in the rodeo events. On the range a chute is used for branding, veterinary attention, segregating animals, etc.

The **bucking horses** used in rodeos, are naturally inclined to unseat their riders, but to assure that they put on a good show, a **bucking cinch** or **flank cinch** is placed well to the rear around his belly to stimulate bucking.

172

SUNFISHER

Sunfishing refers to the motion of a bucking horse when he sways and twists from side to side as he jumps so that his forefeet land alternately on opposite sides of his line of progress. This motion, added to the bucking, makes it particularly difficult for the rider to stay aboard.

In **bronc riding** contests only one hand may be used and the rider is required to "scratch" his horse, that is, spur him alternately on the flanks and shoulders. The bronc rider is required to stay on a bucking horse **ten seconds** if he is in a saddle—**eight seconds** if bareback.

In bronc riding contests, a mounted **pick up man** is also in the arena. It is his job to release the bucking cinch and lift the contestant off the bucking horses when the time limit has expired.

Contests usually included in a rodeo are: saddle bronc riding, bareback bronc riding, steer riding, bulldogging (steer wrestling), calf roping, steer roping, team roping and steer decorating (tieing a ribbon on horn or tail).

In **bulldogging** contests a **hazer** assists the contestants by galloping on the opposite side of the steer to keep it from veering away when the contestant slips out of his saddle to tie it down.

Famous summer rodeos are the **Stampede** at Calgary, Canada; the **Roundup** at Pendleton, Oregon; **Frontier Days** at Cheyenne, Wyoming.

The most important winter rodeo is generally considered to be the **World's Championship Rodeo** at Madison Square Garden in New York City.

Rodeos generally are classified with respect to the amount of prize money offered.

The **Rodeo Association of America**, organized in 1928, establishes the rules and regulations and is the governing body for all official rodeos.

173

HORSE SHOWS—Many horse shows offer a **Western Division**, generally in two parts—a stock horse section and a pleasure horse section.

Classes may include stock horses—lightweight, heavyweight and open, junior stock horses, ladies stock horses, a jaquima class (horses not more than five years old, never ridden in other than a snaffle bit bridle and usually shown in a bosal), western trail horses, western pleasure horses and a western pair class. The horses shown in Western Divisions may be any breed or combination of breeds, 14.1 hands and over of stock horse type—stallions, mares and geldings.

Faults include a switching tail, exaggerated opening of mouth, hard or heavy mouth, lugging, nervous throwing of head, falling or hesitating while being shown, particularly anticipating being checked.

Good characteristics include good manners, a shifty and smooth performance with feet under the horse at all times, particularly when stopping, a soft mouth and ready response to a light rein, especially when turning, head maintained in a natural position, speed while under the control of the rider, and ability to gallop and lope on the correct lead.

In Western classes, **points** are scored as follows. When not worked on cattle: response to the reins—50 points; conformation—20 points; manners—20 points; appointments—10 points. When worked on cattle: a total of 150 points; cow work—50 points; response to the reins—50 points; conformation—20 points; manners—20 points; and appointments —10 points. Western trail horses: performance and manners—60 points; appointments, equipment and neatness—20 points; conformation—20 points. Western pleasure horses: performance—60 points; conformation —30 points; appointments—10 points. Western pair class: performance —50 points; conformation—25 points; tack and equipment—25 points. Stock horses are worked individually.

In **showing** stock horses, the rider is required to use only *one hand* and the hand may not be changed. The hand must be around the reins (fingers must not be between the reins) and the rider's hands must be clear of the horse and saddle while the horse is in motion.

Appointments include a stock saddle without Tapaderos, western bridle and bit, and riders must wear western hat, chaps, cowboy boots and carry a rope or riata. Prohibited are spurs and bosals, cavesson nosebands, martingales, choke ropes, tie downs, and metal chin straps.

SOME HISTORY AND GENERAL INFORMATION—The **Pony Express** was a private company which operated a relay of horses to carry mail from St. Joseph, Missouri to San Francisco, California before railroads were extended across the country. It was started in April 1860.

Famous painters of Western scenes, horses and men include: Charles

M. Russell, Frederick Remington, William Ziegler, Pete Martinez, Burris Jenkins, Frank Hoffman, William R. Leigh and Olaf Weighorst.

Will James was a well-known cowboy artist and author.

Will Rogers was a famous cowboy comedian and philosopher.

The surname of **Buffalo Bill** (the famous Indian Fighter) was **Cody**.

Other countries, besides the United States, noted for their range cattle and horses are **Canada** and **Argentina**.

THE CATTLE RIDERS OF LATIN AMERICA—The **vaquero** of Mexico, the **gaúcho** of Brazil, the **llanero** of Venezuela, the **huaso** of Chile, the **gaucho** of Argentina and Uruguay, and the North American **cowboy**, are as much alike as Ford cars off the same assembly line. They all learned their methods of cattle handling, branding, roping, and the like, from the same source—Spain—and their herds and the horses they rode were, in the beginning, descended from those brought over by the Conquistadores. These horsemen became folk-heroes in their various countries and national symbols of courage, virility, and the spirit of independence: while each group also inspired a regional literature of great and continuing popularity.

SADDLES AND GEAR—The ring bit and the saddles they rode with the tall pommels and high cantles were, with one exception, copies of those the Arabs brought to Spain and, later, the Conquistadores took with them to the New World. The only change was an added horn for roping. On the pampas there was no wood to make saddle trees, so the gaucho adopted a sort of layer-cake arrangement, in use in Southern Spain, made up of sweat cloths, leather, and woolly sheep skins, piled one on the other, and held in place by an overall girth. As it had no horn, the gaucho was forced to make fast the end of his **reata** to the cinch ring. The llanero of Venezuela used a different method. He sometimes plaited his lasso into the hair of his horse's tail, which took the entire shock of stopping a roped steer.

The Mexicans adopted the wooden tree of the Conquistadores, and added a very large wooden horn: but, when the cowboys learned the cattle business from them, they substituted a much smaller metal horn, which permitted them to make a quicker **dally** (several turns of the reata around the horn).

FACON—The **facon** was the long sheath-knife every gaucho carried stuck in the back of his belt. It was the pampas tool chest, for with it he slaughtered and skinned cattle, carved out thongs of rawhide to make or mend his gear, cut his meat, picked his teeth, and even fought his duels with his poncho wrapped around his arm as a sort of buckler.

BOLEADORAS—The early Spaniards took over this weapon from the Indians who invented it. It consisted of three rawhide thongs some six feet long. Three ends were fastened together and a round weight the size of a billiard ball, and originally made of stone, was attached to each of the other ends. Holding one ball in his hand and swinging the other two around his head, the horseman galloped after his prey—horse, cow, or rhea, as the case might be. When close enough he flung his weapon which entangled the animal's legs and threw it.

TROPILLA—This is the gaucho term for his string of horses—his **remuda**. He chooses eight to fourteen geldings (no self-respecting son of the pampas would ever ride a mare) as much alike in conformation and color as possible, and adds a pinto **bell-mare** because she is more easily visible at night. Then each horse in turn is neck-yoked to the mare until they become friends and he will follow her anywhere. Leading his bell-mare and with his **tropilla** following, the gaucho can make phenomenal rides; when the horse under him tires, he stops, and, at his whistle, all the mounts line up while he saddles a fresh one and then continues on his way.

GAUCHO GAMES—The gauchos' rough, equestrian sports have helped to make him a superb horseman. He will, for instance, permit a friend to **boleador** his horse as he rides by at full gallop. Then, when the animal turns turtle, if he fails to land on his feet like a cat with the reins in his hand, he loses his reputation and becomes the butt of jokes.

Another game was known as **el pato** (the duck). A large group of gauchos on their fastest mounts would gather at a **pulpería**, or pampas pub, and shout: "*pato! pato!*" until its owner brought out a live duck sewn up in a rawhide bag with four stout grips. Mounted men each grasped a handle and, at the word, the strongest pulled the pato away from the others and started off across the pampas at a wild gallop with the entire pack following, each rider trying to snatch the duck away. The one who finally reached the appointed **estancia** carrying it under his arm was adjudged the winner.

So many pedestrians and animals were left a bloody pulp on the pampas in the wake of these galloping hordes, and so many fatal fights occurred among the contestants, that pato was declared illegal for a long time. But lately it has been revived as a sort of basketball on horseback with strict rules.

Probably the wildest feat of all, and, as far as I know, performed nowhere else, is **el salto de la maroma**, which takes its name from the crossbeam that connects the tops of the gateposts of a corral. The performer sits on this bar and, as a bunch of bare-backed broncos rush through the open gates, he drops on one and lets it buck and run for awhile. Then he begins to fan it on one side of its head with his hat until the bronco turns back toward the corral. When it reaches there,

he brings the heavy end of his quirt down hard between the horse's ears, knocking it to its knees, and then dismounts.

The pampas spawned a rawhide-tough race of horsemen, many of mixed Spanish and Indian blood, that fought the Indians, pushed forward the frontier, laid the foundation for a great cattle empire, and formed the backbone of the armies that repulsed the British, defeated the Portuguese, and eventually wrested Latin America from Spanish domination.

(Edward Larocque Tinker)

THE CAVALRY—The cavalry is no more. But it has a glorious past. It was the elite corps of the Army because it was small and because, throughout the ages, glamor has surrounded the horseman; in any age, at any time, he is a knight in shining armor wearing a bright plume!

Perhaps the **most famous poem** lauding the valor, color and courage of the cavalry is Lord Tennyson's "Charge of the Light Brigade" (an action of British Cavalry against the Russians in the Crimean War in 1854). Probably the best known stanza is:

> *"Forward, the Light Brigade!"*
> *Was there a man dismayed?*
> *Not though the soldiers knew*
> *Some one had blundered:*
> *Theirs not to make reply,*
> *Theirs not to reason why,*
> *Theirs but to do and die;*
> *Into the valley of Death*
> *Rode the six hundred.*

The **insignia** of the Cavalry was crossed sabers (the hilt down).

The Cavalry's **color** was yellow.

The national and organization flags carried by the Cavalry and other mounted troops were known as **standards** rather than "colors."

The U. S. Army does not now, of course, and did not always, include Horse Cavalry. Mounted troops were not continuously maintained as part of our Army until 1833. Such mounted troops as were organized prior to that time were generally known as Dragoons.

The three regiments of cavalry and one of dragoons authorized by Congress shortly after the independence of the United States were never at their authorized strength and were subsequently disbanded, so that between 1802 and the beginning of the War of 1812 our army included no mounted troops. The two regiments of dragoons authorized, and partially organized just prior to the War of 1812, were disbanded in 1815.

The 1st U. S. Cavalry Regiment was organized in 1833 as the Regiment of Dragoons; its designation was changed to the 1st U. S. Cavalry (Regiment) in 1861. The 4th Cavalry Regiment was designated the 1st Cavalry in 1855 and changed back to the 4th Cavalry in 1861.

A "Mounted Riflemen" regiment was voted by Congress in 1845 as part of a program of frontier defense. Military posts were to be established along the trail to Oregon. The Mexican War broke out before this Regiment could take up its posts and it served in Mexico before settling the Oregon Trail.

The U. S. Cavalry was prominent in the Civil War (as was the Cavalry of the Confederate States), in the Indian Wars (Custer's last stand) and in the Spanish War in Cuba.

Virtually, there was no mounted Cavalry in World Wars I and II. However, a provisional squadron of the 2nd Cavalry Regiment participated in mounted action in the Saint Mihiel and Meuse-Argonne operations during World War I, and the 26th U. S. Cavalry (Philippine Scouts) were in mounted action on Bataan in the Philippine Islands during World War II. During the early days of World War II, the 1st and 2nd Cavalry Divisions and the 112th and 124th Cavalry Regiments were organized, trained and equipped as horse Cavalry until they left for overseas assignments. During World War I, most of the Cavalry units were converted to horse-drawn field artillery. During World War II, Cavalry were converted variously to mechanized reconnaissance regiments or groups, armored units and infantry. The 1st Cavalry Division—consisting of the 7th, 8th, 5th and 12th Regiments, supporting artillery and other divisional troops—fought dismounted as infantry as an element of the Sixth Army, distinguishing itself in the Southwest Pacific on the Admiralty Islands and in the Philippines. It was first in Manila and first in Tokyo. Although all of its combat operations were in the role of infantry, the Division retained its Cavalry designation throughout.

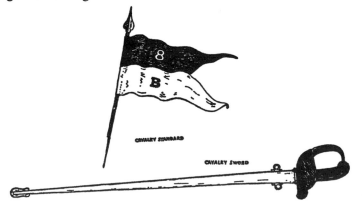

CAVALRY STANDARD

CAVALRY SWORD

The cavalry regiments of our Army have been designated Dragoons and Mounted Rifles as well as Cavalry—but it has never contained any **Hussars** or **Lancers.**

Hussars were light cavalry armed with a saber and often distinguished by brilliant uniforms.

Lancers were light cavalry armed with lances.

Dragoons were cavalry equipped for fighting on foot, and often did so. They were in effect mounted infantry.

PERSONALITIES—The first Chief of Cavalry was Major General Willard A. Holbrook. The last was Major General John K. Herr.

Famous U. S. Cavalry Commanders include: William Woods Averell, John Buford, George A. Custer, D. M. Gregg, Benjamin H. Grierson, Hugh Judson Kilpatrick, Ranald S. Mackenzie, Wesley Merritt, Alfred Pleasanton, Philip H. Sheridan, George Stoneman, John Moulder Wilson, John J. Pershing, Willis D. Crittenberger, E. N. Harmon, Kenyon Joyce, Geoffrey Keyes, Ben Lear, John Milliken, George S. Patton, Innis P. Swift, Lucian K. Truscott, Jonathan M. Wainwright.

Famous Confederate Cavalry Commanders include: Bedford Forrest, Fitzhugh Lee, W. H. F. ("Rooney") Lee, John Hunt Morgan, Thomas Lafayette Rosser, J. E. B. ("Jeb") Stuart, Joe Wheeler, Turner Ashby.

ORGANIZATION—For many years the seat of Cavalry activities was at **Fort Riley**, Kansas, location of the Cavalry School. Prominent also was **Fort Bliss**, Texas, home of the 1st Cavalry Division.

At its greatest strength, the regular horse Cavalry, consisted of two Divisions, the 1st and 2nd and (including regiments in the Divisions) 18 regiments the 2nd through 12th, 14th and 26th (Philippine Scouts). (The 1st and 13th Cavalry Regiments were the first to be converted to armor.)

The **Cavalry Division** was somewhat smaller than the infantry division, approximately 11,000 officers and men; the **Cavalry Regiment** about half the size of the infantry regiment, approximately 1500 officers and men.

The horse cavalry before it was disbanded included in its **arms** the following weapons: rifle, pistol, light machine gun, heavy machine gun, 37 mm gun (one pounder), .50 caliber air-cooled machine gun (anti-tank), 81 mm mortar, carbine, sub-machine gun (Tommy gun) and rocket launcher ("bazooka"). The saber as a weapon was abandoned in 1933.

The **Regiment** comprised two squadrons (corresponding to infantry battalions) and the squadrons were, in turn, sub-divided into **troops** (each corresponding to an infantry company). In addition, the regiment contained several separate troops (machine gun, special weapons, headquarters, and service). Just prior to the deactivation of the cavalry, a rifle troop consisted of seven officers and 166 men—a rifle platoon of one officer and 28 men.

183

The chief **characteristic** of cavalry was its unusual cross-country mobility combined with fire power and the capability of surprise shock action.

Missions assigned cavalry were reconnaissance; counter reconnaissance; advance, rear and flank guard; raiding; exploitation of victories (pursuit); the seizing of ground and holding it until infantry arrived; delaying action, etc.

The mounted cavalry trooper was armed with a rifle and pistol. The distinctive cavalry sword was abandoned in 1933.

THE CAVALRY HORSE—The U. S. **Cavalry Mount** was generally one-half or more Thoroughbred—usually by Thoroughbred sires out of light or medium weight mares of the Thoroughbred type and a good infusion of that blood. However, there were also some Morgans, Arabs and Standardbreds. Both mares and geldings were used. Cavalry mounts were obtained by purchase through remount agents, largely in the western and southern states. They were usually horses sired by Government stallions.

The **price** paid by the Government for cavalry mounts averaged in the order of $165—and did not exceed $200. In general, cavalry mounts averaged 15.2 hands in **height** and about 1,000 pounds in **weight**.

The Army mount was easily identified by the **Preston brand** on its neck (on the near side). This consisted of three numerals with a preceding or following letter. (There was both a **WOOO** and an **OOOW**.)

At the peak of World War II, the Army had about 21,000 **mules**—largely in the China-Burma Theater and in Italy and in the Alps. These were obtained by purchase from private breeders. (The Army helped by providing farmers with suitable jacks.) Mules were used primarily as pack animals in units trained to operate in mountainous and other difficult country. They were also used as dray animals in the normal "housekeeping" of posts, camps and stations.

A **remount** was a new, young or "recruit" horse—one not yet trained to the prescribed standard or finally assigned as a trooper's mount. The Army operated three **remount stations** (breeding and training establishments) at Fort Reno, Oklahoma; Fort Robinson, Nebraska; and Front Royal, Virginia.

The **loss of animals** in all wars has been very great. During the Civil War, in 1864, the Federal Army required more than 500 horses each day to replace losses. During the first eight months of 1864 the Cavalry of the Army of the Potomac used up 40,000 horses—an average of two remounts to each man. During the Russian Campaign of 1812, Napoleon crossed the Niemen with 187,000 horses. Six months later he recrossed the Niemen with 1600 horses.

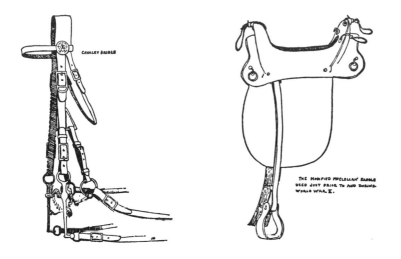

THE MODIFIED MCCLELLAN SADDLE
USED JUST PRIOR TO AND DURING
WORLD WAR I.

TACK—The most distinctive item of equipment in our Cavalry was the famous and long used **McClellan saddle**. This was a slight modification of the stock or western saddle; it had no pommel horn, but a rather prominent pommel and cantle and fitted over a folded blanket. It was designed to carry a pack on the pommel and cantle, a rifle and saber; the stirrups were hooded. If properly adjusted, it was easy on the horse's back and unlikely to give him saddlesores. It looked like this—

Officers generally used a "Flat" or "English" saddle with extended cantle panels. This was the **Saumur** saddle. (The official name was Officers' Field Saddle.) Cavalry officers also used a nearly conventional "Flat" saddle known as the Phillips Training Saddle.

Cavalry **bridles** contained a bit and bridoon, both suspended from the same cheekstrap. A halter shank clipped to the bridle and fastened around the horse's neck—in appearance like a Martingale—was also standard equipment.

THE PACK—The trooper's pack weighed about 65 pounds; it was carried in a pommel roll, a cantle roll and in two saddle bags. These, in addition to the Cavalryman's rifle and pistol (and earlier, his sword) and the weight of the trooper himself, comprised the cavalry mount's load. Cavalry pack horses carried about 250 pounds.

MARCHES AND GAITS—The longest peacetime march made in a day by horse cavalry with full equipment, terminating with the command in good condition, was—believe it or not—100 miles! This record one-day march was made by the Cavalry School Brigade, Fort Riley, Kansas in the spring of 1931 and again in the spring of 1932. A satis·

185

factory day's march for trained horse cavalry with full equipment was, however, only about 35 miles.

Cavalry marches are generally made at the rate of about six miles per hour—at the trot and walk—with at least a five-minute halt each hour.

Cavalry horses were trained to:

Walk at 4 miles per hour. **Trot** at 9 miles per hour (and at times 8 miles per hour). **Gallop collected** at 12 miles per hour. **Gallop extended** at 16 (or more) miles per hour.

A march at the rate of six miles per hour, on a good road, would include trotting 30 minutes, walking 25 minutes and halting 5 minutes. This would be accompiished roughly in this order: trot 6 minutes and walk 4 or 3; e.g., Walk 5; trot 6; walk 3; trot 6 and walk 4; three times; trot 6; walk 3; lead 2; halt 5. (Total 1 hour.)

FOREIGN CAVALRY SCHOOLS—Many United States Cavalry officers attended foreign cavalry schools to broaden their education and bring back new ideas for development in the United States. These foreign cavalry schools were:

Italy	Pinerolo and Tor di Quinto
France	Saumur
Germany	Hannover
England	Weedon
Austria	Vienna

FAMOUS AMERICAN CAVALRY GUARD ORGANIZATIONS

First Troop Philadelphia City Cavalry. Organized as the Light Horse of Philadelphia Novembei 17, 1774. The "City Troop" is the oldest active military unit in continuous service in the United States.

Squadron A (Originally Troop A) was officially mustered into the New York National Guard April 2, 1889. It had its origins in a mounted group organized in New York City during the Blaine-Cleveland Campaign in the summer of 1884.

PURPOSE—The primary purpose of mounted police, which are found in all large cities and seldom anywhere else, is to control riots and heavy traffic and to patrol public parks. Also, when the occasion demands it, they act as mounted escorts to dignitaries and participate in parades. They are most frequently on regular duty in the theater district, congested shopping districts, the waterfront and at railroad and truck terminals.

MOUNTS—The distinguishing characteristic of police mounts is that, in any city or sub-group of the police of any city, they are uniform in size, weight and color. They are trained for their work and to be calm under conditions which might excite most horses, well mannered and courageous—and they possess reasonable stamina. Police horses, of course, must do a great deal of standing. They trot very little and gallop seldom. They must be used to people coming up to them suddenly, shouting at them or their rider, all kinds of noises, flashing lights, automobiles coming toward them, behind them and too close to them—and people petting them, giving them apples, carrots and sugar.

The height of police mounts is generally between 15.3 and 16.2 hands.

The price paid for police mounts varies considerably, of course, depending on the type of mount desired and proximity to the source. A good average, however, is probably about $300.

SOURCE—The breeding of police mounts is varied—some are Thoroughbreds, some are ¾, ½ and ¼ breds, some have saddle horse or Morgan backgrounds, others are from the Western Plains—specific origin is unknown. In general, most city police departments have a contract with horse dealers to procure for them the required number of suitable mounts at an average price. Specifications usually include sex (the New York City Police Department uses only geldings), height, weight, color and general type or breeding—all within reasonable limits.

In many instances, horses are given to the police by interested benefactors and admirers. Many of these are Thoroughbreds that have proved not quite fast enough for the track; and hunters and saddle horses whose owners want to find a good home for mounts which, for one reason or another, they no longer wish to maintain.

New horses (remounts) joining the force are usually given initial training by a small group of specialists known as the Remount Group. After the remounts are broken, handled and have become reasonably tractable, they are assigned to an experienced mounted policeman who continues the horse's training, on and off patrol.

TACK—The tack used by most police organizations is similar to that formerly used by the United States Cavalry. Usually the bits are of the double (bit and bridoon) type, brow bands are colored and the rosettes bear the city's coat of arms. Sometimes white halter shanks are attached to the bridle—seldom are martingales used. The saddle is usually the United States Army's McClellan saddle or some slight variation of it like the Whitman saddle used by the New York City Police. Therefore, pads or folded blankets are usual under the saddle and many police organizations use hooded stirrups. In wintertime, police horses frequently wear blankets on patrol.

STABLING—Stabling is usually in rented quarters—armories, riding stables, warehouse space not used for other purposes, etc. Necessarily, most of the horses are stabled in standing (straight) stalls rather than boxes. However, the horse's daily duties and exercise periods make this no hardship.

MEN—Policemen assigned to mounted work frequently, of course, have had some experience with horses; but perhaps an even greater number have had simply a strong desire to join the mounted service. Most police forces are glad to have recruits without previous association with horses and start them off with the fundamentals of horsemanship—continuing to educate them through as much advanced work as is required.

Each police trooper takes care of his own mount—trains him, grooms him, exercises him and looks after his general comfort. Hostlers water and feed the horses, clean their stalls and bed them down.

HOURS OF DUTY—In most police organizations, the patrolmen are on mounted duty for eight hours—less one hour for a meal. However, they spend extra time looking after their mounts and tack, studying and performing special duties.

ORGANIZATION—These days mounted police detachments are relatively small and, again, vary considerably throughout the cities that use them. In New York, there are approximately 250 mounted patrolmen and horses organized into six troops. With officers and clerical personnel, the total assigned one way or another to the mounted detachment in New York City numbers some 300.

SUMMONSES AND ARRESTS—The usual violations for which mounted policemen issue summonses and make arrests are traffic violations, disorderly conduct, disturbing the peace, inciting riots, etc.

MOUNTED ESCORT

There are no rules for mounted escorts, but several sound principles. Most important are these:

UNIFORMITY—The horses used should be of generally uniform appearance in height, weight, conformation, color and type. The bridles and saddles should be the same or at least very similar. All or none should use blankets or pads and, if blankets or pads are used, they should be uniform in design, color and shape. All should wear halter shanks or martingales—or none should. If halter shanks are used, the rope should be of good quality and whitewashed.

The riders, of course, should be in an appropriate uniform.

DIGNITY—A mounted organization or detachment should take its work seriously. It is a dignified assignment and dignity is called for. With dignity, come cleanliness and sparkle—"spit and polish." Horses should be well groomed, their hoofs oiled; tack should be clean and metal parts should glisten. Uniforms of the riders should be well fitting, clean and pressed—the men should be shaven. Commands should be clear and crisp, and there should be no more than are necessary for control. There should be no talking in ranks.

FORMATIONS SUITABLE TO THE OCCASION—Regular cavalry formation—line, columns of 2's, 3's, 4's, 6's or 8's—or a diamond may be used as such, or modified to suit the occasion. Sometimes the mounted unit will march as a unit in a specific place in the parade. At other times, a portion of it will precede, while another portion follows motor vehicles or people on foot. On some occasions, a small group may flank motor vehicles.

The parade marshal generally will have a pretty good idea of what he wants in and from a mounted detachment. If the capabilities and limitations of the mounted group permit it, the marshal's directions are followed. If his desires appear impractical or beyond the capabilities of the mounted group—or his plan does not appear to use the mounted group to its greatest effectiveness—he should be informed of this with a positive suggestion for a better use of the mounted group.

PRECISION—When joining a parade, persons to be escorted during the parade, at any change of formation, and on leaving, the mounted detachment should form, move and conduct itself with precision, military bearing and order.

ABILITY—Be sure that the horses and men selected are up to the job required of them. The impression made by a mounted escort is easily spoiled by fractious horses and also by laggards (especially unduly pokey ones). Certainly poor and careless riding, unmilitary bearing, improperly adjusted tack and, of course, lack of cleanliness, make perhaps an even worse impression. Pick your horses and men for the job.

PLANNING—The simplest worthwhile effort requires planning. This means a full and accurate knowledge of what is to be done. Consideration is given to how it will be accomplished, what formation is best, where the group will meet and be dismissed; by what means, with what personnel, and the source of these; who will be responsible for what, who will get what, who will check what; how much practice is required, where and when it will be held, where the group will meet, how members will be kept informed; and so on and so on, through a myriad of details.

There is only one way to do this. Make out a list of things to be done, who will do them, when they should be completed and who will check progress and see that each job is properly completed on time.

PRACTICE—Practice, of course, makes perfect; but there is seldom time for enough practice to assure perfection. Some practice, however, is necessary. Plan for this and do it. You have got to put on a good show and you must have some practice to do this.

RESPONSIBILITY—Responsibility must be clearly established. There must be a responsible head of the group. He, in turn, should designate the responsibilities of key individuals and they, in turn, the responsibilities of others. The responsibility and chain of command having been established, all must cooperate in observing and respecting it.

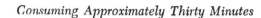

MOUNTED DRILL

Consuming Approximately Thirty Minutes

Fall In.
Count fours.
Anyone who feels incapable of riding at No. 1 or 4, change positions.

Fours right, March.
Column right, March,
Column of twos, March.
Column of troopers, March.
Column of fours, March.
Column of troopers, March.

Trot, March.
Column of twos, March.
Column of fours, March.
Column of troopers, March.
Change hands. (At the next corner, the column moves diagonally across the arena and changes direction.)

Walk, March.
Release stirrups.
Slow trot, March (Once around ring).
Walk, March.
Half-turn.
Troopers circle to the left.
Half-turn and reverse.
Half-turn.
Troopers circle to the right.
Half-turn and reverse.
Take stirrups.

From front to rear count threes.
Trot, March.
By threes, by the left flank, March (Track right at end of hall).
By threes, by the right flank, March (Track left at end of hall).

Column of fours, March.
Walk, March.
Fours left, March.
Troop, Halt.
Column of fours from the right, Trot March.
Column right, March.
Column of twos, March.
Column of troopers, March.

(At the middle of one end of the ring) Column Right, March.
(At opposite end of ring) Troopers left and right.
Columns half left and half right (When leading troopers on each side reach end of ring. This produces a cross-over or criss-cross in the center of the ring).
Columns half left and half right (Double back).

(At end of ring) Column of twos.
Twos, left and right.
(Twos) Columns half left and half right (Criss-cross).

193

(Twos) Columns half left and half right (Double back).

(At end of ring) Column of fours.
Fours, left and right.
(Fours) Columns half left and half right (Criss-cross).
(Fours) Columns half left and half right (Double back).

(Caution—"Even fours left, odd fours right".)

(At end of ring) Line, March.
Walk, March.
Troop, Halt.
Lead out from the right and ride at will—cool your horses.

NOTE: If desired, with an advanced group, movements indicated at a walk may be at a trot and those indicated at a trot may be at a canter (collected gallop).

A T E S T O F H O R S E M A N S H I P

DISMOUNTED

1. **Nomenclature:** Bring in a horse:
   a. Ask the individual to point to the following:
   Muzzle, hocks, loins, fetlock, cannon, knee, elbow, withers, croup, dock, forearm, point of the shoulder, coronet, gaskin, frog, pastern, bars of the jaw, stifle, chestnut, poll.
   b. Ask him to point out 10 additional parts of the horse.
2. **Types and conformation:** Bring in horses of whatever types are available. Then for each ask:
   a. What type of horse is this?
   b. "Fault" him. (Point out his defects in relation to the characteristic conformation and quality of his type.) Include at least: Head, eyes, neck, shoulder, withers, back, pasterns, hoofs, the "top line," height and weight.

194

3. **Colors and markings:** Bring in horses of varied colors and markings.
   a. Have the individual name, or each of the group write, the color of each horse. If any of the following colored horses are not present, have students describe them: Black, brown, bay, liver chestnut, light chestnut, gray, piebald, skewbald, blue roan, red roan, dun.
   b. Have the individual describe, or each of the group write, the distinctive markings of each horse. If any of the following are not present, have students describe them: Blaze, race, star, snip, flecks, dapples, stockings, Preston brand, other brands.

4. **Recognition of common diseases and faults:** If available, bring in a horse or horses with common diseases and conformation defects; if none is available, bring in any horse.
   a. Point to the location and indicate the nature of the following: Curb, spavin, splint, sidebone, ringbone, thrush, capped hock, ophthalmia, thoroughpin, windpuffs, wind colic.
   b. Describe what is meant by: Cowhocked, swaybacked, tied in below the knee, ewe-necked, star gazer, herring gutted, goose rumped, forging, Roman nosed, splayfooted.

5. **Age:** If available, bring in horses of the following ages: 2 to 4, 5 to 7, 8 to 9, 10 to 14, 15 to 20.
   a. What is the age of each of these horses?
      (1) Why do you think so?
   b. What, in general, is the characteristic appearance of the teeth of a horse that is:

4 years old?	6 years old?	8 years old?
10 years old?	15 years old?	20 years old?

6. **Stable management:** Bring in a horse; provide a section of picket line or stable area with tie ring; bridle, saddle and cleaning material for horse and tack.
   a. Tie the horse
      (1) To the picket line,
      (2) To the ring.
   b. Have student demonstrate:
      (1) How to brush the near side.
      (2) How to brush the off side.
      (3) Use of a rub rag.
      (4) Use of a scraper.
      (5) Use of a hoof pick.
      (6) Use of the comb on the tail and mane.
   c. Where should a curry comb not be used?
   d. Indicate how a twitch is used.

e. Hobble the horse.

f. Pick up the horse's:
   (1) Near forefoot,
   (2) Off hindfoot

g. Approximately what daily quantity of each of the following would you feed a middle weight riding horse in good condition, working regularly: (1) Oats? (2) Hay? (3) Bran? (4) Salt? (5) Greens? (6) Corn?

h. How much straw bedding should a horse have, the first time new bedding is used?

i. Is fresh straw or old straw better for bedding? Why?

j. How is a bran mash made? How often is it fed?

k. Where a trough is used, in general, how many times a day should a horse be watered? At what times? Just before or after feeding?

l. Approximately how often should a horse be shod?

m. If the time for a horse to be reshod arrives, but his shoes are not worn, what should be done?

n. What is the essence of a good stable?

o. Demonstrate how to clean:
   (1) A bridle,
   (2) A saddle.

p. Name the parts of:
   (1) The bridle,
   (2) The saddle.

7. **Bridling and saddling:** Have a horse in his stall, haltered and tied and a bridle (Pelham) and saddle at hand—the head stall, cavesson and girth incorrectly adjusted, the curb chain hooked on both sides, stirrup irons down.

   a. Bridle and saddle this horse. (Check that curb chain is released before bridling, manner of opening mouth, proper adjustments, etc.)

   b. Assume you have come in from an hour's normal riding. Untack this horse, put him in his stall, place the tack properly in the tack room. (Check that curb chain is released, stirrups run up, girth properly cared for, bit cleaned, underside of saddle and girth are cleaned, etc.)

MOUNTED

1. Mount. (Observe that adjustment of bridle, saddle and girth is checked, that near rein is tightened, correctness, alacrity and ease of mounting.)

2. Shorten the off stirrup one hole without removing the foot from the stirrup.

3. Tighten the girth while in the saddle.
4. Dismount.
5. **Walk**, Halt, Extended Walk; Halt, Back.
6. **Trot**, Walk, Halt, Trot Extended changing diagonals twice; Slow Trot; Trot a figure 8 (posting) and change diagonals in each loop; Slow trot without stirrups in a figure 8.
7. **Canter** (right lead)—Trot, Canter (left lead), Walk, Canter (right lead), Halt. Figure 8 (check correctness of leads). Release stirrups on command while cantering a figure 8, Halt.
Have rider canter in a straight line, naming the lead on which he will depart and then change leads.
8. **Gallop** to a designated point, turn sharply about, right handed; gallop to the starting point, turn sharply about left handed; gallop on to a designated point and halt abruptly.
9. **Jump** 3 feet, twice (check form, control of horse, etc.).

NOTE: A thirteen-year-old boy who had not had previous experience, after about four hours instruction a week, over a six months period, passed this test with a score of 96 percent.

HORSE ORGANIZATIONS

The following is an outline of National Horse Organizations not included elsewhere in this book.

THE UNITED STATES PONY CLUBS

The **United States Pony Clubs, Inc.,** 53 State Street, Boston 9, Massachusetts, is a national organization to promote the riding and care of horses and ponies by those under 21 years of age.

The **purpose** is to develop and encourage among children throughout the United States a knowledge of riding and horsemanship, including the care of horses and ponies; to encourage fair and friendly competition; to develop in the rider understanding of and sympathy for the horse; and by these and other means to develop in young riders strength of character, alert minds and sound bodies.

The **organization** consists of a national headquarters with affiliated local member clubs in various parts of the country. It is administered by a Board of Governors which is represented in each state by a Regional Supervisor having general supervision of all member clubs within that state. It is also represented by Visiting Commissioners who are available to carry out special assignments for the Board throughout the entire country.

Active **membership** is approximately 3,500—900 boys and 2,600 girls. Sustaining members (over 21) number about 600. There are about 85 clubs in 24 states.

Sponsored events include regional and national rallies and rated tests of performance for its members.

Identification of members: A distinctive blue, white and gold pin.

THE UNITED STATES EQUESTRIAN TEAM, INC.

The **United States Equestrian Team, Inc.**, Warrenton, Virginia, is a non-profit organization devoted to the support and training of teams to represent this country in the field of international equestrian competition. The U.S.E.T. works closely with the U. S. Olympic Committee, the U. S. Olympic Equestrian Committee, the U. S. Combined Training Association, the Pan American Games Committee and the American Horse Shows Association.

The **purpose** is to develop horses and riders to represent the United States in international competition in Dressage, the Three Day Event and *Prix des Nations* jumping.

The **organization** consists of a national headquarters in New York City and the office of the Executive Vice President and Treasurer in Warrenton, Virginia. It is administered by the officers and an Executive Committee which represents the Board of Directors. Activities and administration are decentralized into 10 geographical zones in the United States with a Vice President in charge of each. The 75 member Board of Directors is elected from throughout the 10 zones.

Support is derived from voluntary contributions and donations made by individuals and organizations, such as riding clubs, horse shows, etc.

THE UNITED STATES COMBINED TRAINING ASSOCIATION

The **United States Combined Training Association** is a national non-profit educational association devoted to the combined training of all riders and their horses other than those included in the program for juniors of the U. S. Pony Clubs or in the program for international competition of the U. S. Equestrian Team, Inc.

Members of the Board of Directors represent about 20 combined training events or horse trials, located from Massachusetts to California, which are held under its rules and sanction; which are modified versions of the Olympic Three Day Event; and which include Dressage, Roads and Tracks, Steeplechase, Cross Country and Stadium Jumping phases. The office of the President and Treasurer is 501 George Street, New Brunswick, N. J., the office of the Secretary at Middleburg, Va.

THE UNITED HUNTS RACING ASSOCIATION

The **United Hunts Racing Association**, 300 Park Avenue, New York City 22, New York, is a national organization of sportsmen and sportswomen devoted to the promotion and encouragement of hunt race meetings in the United States, "for sport's sake and better sport."

The **purpose** is to promote and encourage hunt racing and major-course steeplechases in the United States through: (1) providing a paid Field Director to serve at the various hunt race meetings without cost to the local sponsors; (2) issuing, in the form of publicity releases to news media, factual information about the horses that will run; (3) encouraging the revival of timber races by guaranteeing the difference between the purse and $1,000; (4) providing an annual award of cash prizes, a total of $6,600, to the three top horses in each of steeplechasing's three divisions—timber, brush and hurdle; and (5) providing $5,000 worth of insurance on each rider while he is competing in a hunt race meeting—without cost to the sponsors of the meeting or the riders.

The **organization** consists of a President, Vice President, Secretary-Treasurer and Assistant Secretary. There are twelve Directors, four Associate Directors and a Field Director.

Active **membership** consists of approximately 1600 members, many outside the United States. Membership dues are $30 per year.

The organization **assists** some 26 hunt race meetings sponsored by 22 organizations each year.

Identification of members: A distinctive gold and green badge which is changed slightly in design each year.

THE PROFESSIONAL HORSEMEN'S ASSOCIATION OF AMERICA

The **Professional Horsemen's Association of America, Inc.** is a national organization of professional horsemen and horsewomen, associated and junior members. Address: The Secretary, 716 Madison Avenue, New York City.

The **purpose** is to care for needy horsemen and to promote horse activity and interest in the horse. Horse shows, race meets, gymkhana, forums and other events of a similar nature are promoted to increase interest in the horse and produce revenue for the Association.

The **organization** consists of a national headquarters with affiliated branch chapters in various parts of the country. The national organization is governed by a Board of Directors. The officers include a President, Vice-President, Secretary and Treasurer. Each chapter has its own Chairman, Vice-Chairman, Secretary and Treasurer to handle the affairs of its chapter.

Active **membership** is approximately 1,000, including regular, associated and junior memberships.

Members may be **identified** by the PHA's distinctive green and gold pin.

AMERICAN LIVESTOCK

RECORD ASSOCIATIONS

Draft horses

American Cream Draft Horse Association	Hubbard, Iowa
American Shire Horse Association	Hallsville, Mo.
American Suffolk Horse Association, Inc.	Clinton, New Jersey
Belgian Draft Horse Corporation of America	Wabash, Indiana
Clydesdale Breeders Association of the United States	Clarksburg, W. Va.
Percheron Horse Association of America	Fair Oaks, Indiana

Light Horses

American Hackney Horse Society, Inc.	11 Park Place, Room 908 New York 7, New York
American Quarter Horse Association	Amarillo, Texas
American Saddle Horse Breeders Association, Inc.	Louisville, Kentucky
American Appaloosa Association	Chelsea, Oklahoma
Appaloosa Horse Club, Inc.	Moscow, Idaho

Arabian Horse Club Registry of
America, Inc.   111 W. Monroe Street
Chicago 3, Illinois

Cleveland Bay Society of America   White Post, Virginia
The Jockey Club   300 Park Avenue
New York 22, New York

The Morgan Horse Club, Inc.   90 Broad Street
New York 4, New York

Palomino Horse Association, Inc.   Mineral Wells, Texas
Palomino Horse Breeders of America   Reseda, California
Tennessee Walking Horse Breeders' Association of America   Lewisburg, Tennessee
The United States Trotting Association   Columbus, Ohio

Ponies
American Shetland Pony Club   Lafayette, Indiana
Welsh Pony Society of America   Wicomico Church, Va.

Jacks and Jennies
Standard Jack and Jenny Registry
of America   Lexington, Kentucky

ANATOMY, STABLE MANAGEMENT, AILMENTS AND SHOEING

Ellenberger, Wilhelm and others. *Atlas of the Anatomy of Animals for Artists.* Translated and illustrated by Helen Weinbaum. New York: Dover Publications, 1956.

Ensminger, M. M. *Light Horses.* Washington: U. S. Department of Agriculture, 1958.

Hance, J. E. *The Owner Groom.* London: Country Life, Ltd., 1950.

Hayes, M. Horace. *Stable Management.* 2nd Ed. London: Hurst & Blackett, Ltd., 1960.

——. Veterinary Notes for Horse Owners. London: Hurst & Blackett, Ltd., 1959.

Lyon, W. E. *First Aid Hints for the Horse Owner.* London: William Collins Sons & Co., Ltd., 1958.

Orcutt, Henry P. *America's Riding Horses.* Princeton: D. Van Nostrand Co., 1958.

Self, Margaret Cabell. *Horses—Their Selection, Care and Handling*. New York: A. S. Barnes & Co., 1945.

U. S. Department of Agriculture "Yearbook," *Animal Diseases*. Washington, D. C., 1956.

TACK

Carter, William S. H. *Horses, Saddles and Bridles*. Baltimore Press, Baltimore.

Fawcett, William. *Saddle-Room Savings*. New York: Richard R. Smith, Inc., 1931.

McTaggart, M. F. *Stable and Saddle*. London: Methuen & Co., 1937.

Catalogs of Leading Saddlers and Riding Equipment Shops.

EQUITATION AND TRAINING

Chamberlin, Harry D. *Riding and Schooling Horses*. London: Hurst & Blackett, Ltd., 1947.

——. *Training Hunters, Jumpers and Hacks*. London: Hurst & Blackett, Ltd., 1947.

De Sevy, L. *Seat, Gaits and Reactions*. Fort Riley, Ka.: The Cavalry School. 1946.

Dillon, Jane Marshall. *School for Young Riders*. Princeton: D. Van Nostrand Co., 1958.

Horsemanship and Horsemastership. Fort Riley, Ka.: The Cavalry School, 1953.

Littauer, V. S. *Schooling Your Horse*. Princeton: D. Van Nostrand Co., 1956.

Santini, Piero. *The Forward Impulse*. London: Country Life, Ltd., 1951.

Self, Margaret Cabell. *Horsemastership*. New York: A. S. Barnes & Co., 1952.

Seunig, Waldemar. *Horsemanship*. New York: Doubleday & Co., 1956.

Watjen, Richard. *Dressage Riding*. London: J. A. Allen & Co., 1958.

Widmer, Jack. *Practical Horse Breeding and Training*. New York: Charles Scribner's Sons, 1942.

Wiederhold, Hermann. *Your Pony Book*. Brattleboro: Stephen Greene Press, 1958.

Wynmalen, Henry. *Horse Breeding & Stud Management*. London, Country Life, 1950.

HORSE SHOWS

Rule Book, New York: American Horse Show Association. Annual.

Seashole, E. R. *Let's Have A Horse Show*. Atlanta: Consolidated Brands, 1948.

Self, Margaret Cabell. *The American Horse Show*. New York: A. S. Barnes & Co., 1958.

FOXHUNTING

Beckford, Peter. *Thoughts Upon Hunting*. London: Methuen & Co., 1951.
Bowen, Muriel. *Irish Hunting*. Tralee: The Kerrymen Press,
Brock, D. W. E. *Introduction to Foxhunting*. New York: Chas. Scribner's Sons, Inc., 1954.
Burrows, George T. *Gentleman Charles*. London, Vinton & Co., 1951.
Higginson, A. Henry. *Foxhunting—Theory and Practice*. Blue Ridge Press, 1948.
Hull, Dennison B. *Thoughts on American Foxhunting*. New York: David McKay Co., 1958.
James, David and Stephens, Wilson [Ed's.]. *In Praise of Hunting*. London: Hollis & Carter, 1960.
Reeve, J. Stanley. *Foxhunting Formalities*. New York: Derrydale, 1930.
Smith, Thomas. *Extracts from the Diary of a Huntsman*. London: Country Life, Ltd., 1933.
Summerhays, R. S. *Elements of Hunting*. London: Country Life, Ltd., 1938.
Thomas, Joseph B. *Hounds and Hunting through the Ages*. Garden City: Garden City Press, 1937.

BEAGLING

Black, G. G. *American Beagling*. New York: G. P. Putnam's Sons, 1949.
Denlinger, W. M. *The Complete Beagle*. Richmond: Denlinger's, 1956.
Lloyd, J. Ivester. *Beagling*. London: Herbert Jenkins, Ltd., 1954.
Pyper, H. C. *Letters to a Young Beagler*. London: W. H. Allen, 1954.
Whitney, George D. *This is the Beagle*. Garden City: Garden City Press, 1955.

FLAT RACING

American Racing Manual.
Buchanan, Lamont. *Kentucky Derby*. New York: Dutton, 1953.
Burch, Preston M. *Training Thoroughbred Horses*. Lexington: "The Blood Horse," 1958.
Collins, Robert M. *Race Horse Training*. Lexington: "The Blood Horse," 1958.
Hislop, John. *Racing Reflections*. London: Hutchinson & Co., Ltd., 1955.
Palmer, Joe. *This Was Racing*. New York: A. S. Barnes & Co., 1953.
Rules of Racing. New York: The Jockey Club.
Underhill, Tom R. *Thoroughbred Racing and Breeding*. New York: Coward-McCann, Inc., 1945.

STEEPLECHASING

Hislop, John. *Steeplechasing*. London: Hutchinson & Co., Ltd., 1954.

Russell, John E. *History of the Maryland Hunt Cup*. Baltimore: The Sporting Press, 1954.

Rules of Racing. New York: The Jockey Club, Annual.

Steeplechasing in America. New York: National Steeplechase and Hunt Assoc.

HARNESS RACING

Akers, Dwight. *Drivers Up—The Story of American Harness Racing*. New York: G. P. Putnam's Sons, 1958.

Emerson, Eliot. *Fan's Guide to Harness Racing*. New York: Greenberg Co., 1951.

Standardbred Sport. Columbus, Ohio: U. S. Trotting Association.

Wolverton, Clair Cutler. *Fifty Years with Harness Horses*. Harrisburg: Stackpole Co., 1957.

Wrensch, Frank A. *Harness Horse Racing*. Princeton: Van Nostrand, 1948.

POLO

Board, John. *Polo*. New York: A. S. Barnes & Co., 1957.

Bent, Newell. *American Polo*. New York: The Macmillan Co., 1929.

Cullum, Grove. *Selection and Training of the Polo Pony*. New York: Charles Scribner's Sons, 1934.

Devereux, W. B., Jr. *Position and Team Play in Polo*. New York: Brooks Bros., 1914.

McMaster, J. K. *Polo for Beginners and Spectators*. New York: Overstock Book Co., 1954.

U. S. Polo Association Year Book. New York: U. S. Polo Assoc.

Vickers, W. G. *Practical Polo*. London: J. A. Allen & Co., 1959.

COWBOYS AND THE WEST

Fletcher, Sydney E. *The Cowboy and His Horse*. New York: Grosset & Dunlap, Inc., 1951.

Gorman, John A. *The Western Horse: Its Types and Training*. Danville, Illinois: Interstate Printers, 1958.

Sikes, L. N. *Using the American Quarter Horse*. Houston: Saddlerock Corp., 1958.

Young, John Richard. *The Schooling of the Western Horse*. Norman, Okla.: University of Oklahoma Press, 1959.

Widmer, Jack. *The American Quarter Horse*. New York: Charles Scribner's Sons, 1959.

THE CAVALRY

Herr, John K., and Wallace, Edward S. *The Story of the U. S. Cavalry*. Boston: Little Brown & Co., 1953.

R.O.T.C. Cavalry Manual, Basic. Harrisburg: Military Service Publishing Co., 1942.

HISTORICAL

Carter, William Harding. *Horses of the World.* Washington: National Geographic Society, 1923.

Crowell, Pers. *Cavalcade of American Horses.* New York: McGraw-Hill, 1951.

Cunninghame-Graham, R. B. *Horses of the Conquest.* Norman: Univ. of Oklahoma, 1949.

Grigson, Geoffrey [Ed.] *Horse and Rider.* New York: Thames and Hudson, 1950.

Holme, Bryan [Ed.] *Horses.* New York: Studio Publications, 1951.

Hunt, Frazier and Robert. *Horses and Heroes.* New York: Scribners, 1949.

Lamb, A. J. R. *Horse Facts.* Chicago: Ziff-Davis Pub. Co., 1948.

Mochi, Ugo and Carter, T. D., *Hoofed Mammals of the World.* New York: Scribners, 1953.

Stong, Phil. *Horses and Americans.* New York: F. A. Stokes, 1939.

INDEX

Aberdeen Angus cattle, 166
Abortions, 50
Abrasions, first aid for, 41
Across the board, 130
Age, horse's, 4–5
    approximate, determined by teeth, 29–30
"Adios Harry," 141
Aids, riding, 70
Aiken obstacle, 86, 87
Ailments, 41–52
    bibliography, 201
Alert, the, 159–160
Allowance race, 129
Amateur, 84
Amble, 74
American breeds, 11
American Classic, 141
American Derby, 128
American fox hound, 97
American Horse Shows Association (A.H. S.A.), 81
    high score awards, 90
    medal classes, 88
American Kennel Club, 109
American livestock record associations, 200–201
American saddle horse, 10, 11
American Standardbred, 137
American Thoroughbred Stud Book, 132
American trotting horse, 10, 11
Anatomy, 28–32
    bibliography, 201
Anemia, infectious, 48–49
Anthrax, 48
Antiseptics, 50, 51
Antitoxin, tetanus, 51
Anvil, 56
Appaloosa horse, 13
Arabian horse, 9, 12, 81, 184
Arcaro, Eddie, 132
"Aristides," 128
Arroyo, 167
Arthritis, 44
Artists, famous for rendition of horses, 18, 174–175
"Assault," 132
Asses, 8, 9, 13
    domesticated, 9
    wild, 9
Asterisk, before horse's name, meaning of, 131
Attire, beagling and bassetting, 113–114
    cowboys, 170–171
    fox-hunting, 102–105
"Axworthy," 137, 138
"Azucar," 121

Back, sore, 37–38, 47
"Balius," 23
Ball, polo, 145–146
Balding girth, 62, 63, 100
Bandages, 51
    leg, 65
Bar shoe, 55
Bank and rail obstacle, 87
Bar race, 139
Barb, 9, 11
Bareback race, 154
Bassets, 111–112
Bassetting, 109–115
    dress, 113–114
    etiquette, 114
    glossary, 115
    quarries, 109–111

"Battleship," 122
Beagles, 111–112
Beagling, 109–115
    bibliography, 203
    dress, 113–114
    etiquette, 114
    glossary, 115
    quarries, 109–111
Bearing rein, 70, 71
Bedding, 36, 41
Behind the bit, 72–73
Belgian draft horse, 11
Belmont Stakes, 128
Beef cattle, 165–166
"Bellfounder," 138
Bell-mare, 176
Big leg, 45
"Big Red," 132
Billet guards, 100
"Billy," 4
"Billy Direct," 141
Bitch pack, 98
Biting, 37
Bits, 63–64, 99
"Black Hawk," 138
"Blackrod," 142
Blacksmith, 56
Blacktail jackrabbit, 109–110
Blaze (marking), 3
Bleeding, severe, first aid for, 41
Blind staggers, 49
Blindness, 49
Blisters, 51
"Blockade," 122
Blooding hounds, 98
Blowout, 141
Body brush, 36, 37
Bog spavin, 45
Boleadoras, 175–176
Bolting, 50
Bone spavin, 45
Boots, cowboy's, 170–171
    formal hunting, 103
Bosal, 169
Bots, 47
Bowed tendon, 44
Box stalls, dimensions of, 38
Bran mash, 35, 41
Branding, 165, 166, 170, 184
Breaking, 141
Breaking-down, 45
Breast high scent, 96
Breastplate, hunting, 100
Breeches, hunting, 103
Breeding problems, 50
Breeds, 8–14
    American, 11
Breezed under wraps (term defined), 130
Bridles, 63–64
    Cavalry, 185
    Hackamore, 64
    hunting, 99
    Western, 169
Bridling, resisting, 50
Bridoon, 63, 64, 99, 185
Broad jump, 8
Broken wind, 49
Bronc riding contests, 173
Bronchitis, 48
Broncos, 11, 167
Broomtail, 13, 167
Brow band, 63, 99, 190
Bruises, 46
Brush (fox's tail), 96

Brush (hounds), 112
Brush obstacle, 87, 120, 121
Brushes, body, 36, 37
  dandy, 36, 37
Brushing (harness racing term), 140
Brushing, gait and, 32, 50
"Bucephalus," 17
Buckaroo, 167
Bucking cinch, 172
Bucks (male hares), 110
Bucking horses, 172
Buffer, 56, 57
Bulldogging contests, 173
Burro, 9
Byerly Turk, 11, 133

Calf knee, 31
Calks, 55, 147
Canker, 37, 43
Canter, 8, 73, 86
  time required to cover a mile, 6, 7
Cantle, 61
Canvas girth, 62, 63
Cap, hunting, 102, 103
Capped elbow, 44
Capped hock, 44
Cast hounds (term explained), 95
Catalog, horse show, 87
Cataract, 49
Catch weights, 123
Cattle, range, 165–166
Cavalry, U.S., 5, 6, 181–186, 190
  bibliography, 204–205
  marches, 185–186
  missions assigned, 184
  organization, 183–184
  personalities, 128
  tack, 185
Cavalry horses, 184
Cavalry schools, foreign, 186
Cavesson, 63, 99
Cayuse, 13, 167
Celtic pony, 9
Centaur, The, 24
"Chandler," 8
"Change hands," meaning of term, 76
Chape, 96
Chaps, 170
  shotgun, 171
Cheating, 141
Check (fox hunting term), 95
Cheek straps, 63
Chestnuts, 29
Chicken coop obstacle, 86, 87
Children, classification as riders, 84–85
Chincoteague ponies, 12
Chinks, 171
"Christopher Columbus," 149
Chuck wagon, 167
"Chukkers," 146
Chute, 172
Cinch, 169
  bucking (flank), 172
Circus horse, 13
"Citation," 132
Claiming race, 129–130
Classified race, 139
Cleveland Bay, 10
Cloths, saddle, 65
"Clover," 4
Clydesdale draft horse, 11
Coach horses, French, 10
  German, 10
Coat, hunting, 102
Cob, 13
Cold-blooded horse, 11
Colds, 48

Colic, 41, 47
  flatulent, 36, 47
  spasmodic, 47
Colic medicine, 51
Collection, 71
Colon ailments, 47
Colors, horse's, 3
  superstitions about, 21–22
  stable, 65, 131, 132
Colt, 5
Combination saddle horse, 86
"Combination ticket," 130
Combs, curry, 37
Companions, for horses, 5
Conception, 50
Conformation, 31
  faults of, 31
  hunters, 87
Conjunctivitis, 49
Connemara ponies, 9
Contagious equine abortion, 50
Contests, balloon scrimmage, 154
  bronc riding, 173
  bulldogging, 173
  bun eating, 153
  polo ball stroking, 153
  potato picking scramble, 157–158
  removing the saddle, 154
  rodeo, 173
Contracted heels, 43, 55
Cooler, 65
"Copenhagen," 17
Corn horse, 23
Corns, 43
Cottontail rabbit, 110–111
Cougars, 166, 167
Coughing, 48
"Count Fleet," 131
Coupled hounds, 97
Courses, steeplechasing, 120, 121
Covert, 96
  drawing a, 95
  take to, 110
Cow hock, 31
Cowboys, 165–177
  bibliography, 204
Coyotes, 167
Cracked hoof, 43, 55
Creolin, 51
Cribbing, 37, 49
Critter, 167
Cross-country riding, 6–7, 8
Crossed poles obstacle, 86
Crown piece, 63
Cubbing, 95
Cubs, 95
  holding up, 95
Cumberland ponies, 9
Curb bit, 63
Curb chain, 63, 64, 65
Curb reins, 63, 75
Curbs, 44
Curry comb, 36, 37
Cuts, severe, first aid for, 41
Cutting out calves (term defined), 168

Daily double, 130
Dam, 5
"Dan Patch," 142
Dandy brush, 36, 37
Darley Arabian, 11, 133
Dartmouth ponies, 9
Diagonals, changing, 71–72
Diet, 35–36, 37
Direct rein, 70, 71
Direction, changing, 75

Diseases, 41–49
  bibliography, 201
  of foals, 50
Dishing (faulty gait), 31
Disinfectants, 50, 51
Disposition, listless, as sign of sickness, 41
Distemper, 48
Dead heat, 131
Den (fox'es abode), 96
Destruction, humane, 51–52
Devil's horse, 23
Dewlap, 98
Draft horses, breeds of, 11
Drag hounds, 98
Drag hunt, 95
Dragoons, 181, 182, 183
Drawing a covert (term defined), 95
Dress, beagling and bassetting, 113–114
  cowboys, 170–171
  fox hunting, 102–105
Dressage, 74
Dressage seat, 69
Drill, mounted, 193–194
Dropped, see Foaled
Docked (term explained), 4
Dog (male fox), 95
Dog pack, 98
Dogie, 168
Dogtrot, 74
Domesticated horses, 9
Donkeys, 9
Double-back, 110
Double bit, 64, 65
Double bridle, 63, 64, 65
Double-header, 141
Double oxer obstacle, 86
Down-wind, 97
Dude, 168
Dun, Norwegian, 9
Dung, eating, 37

"Eclipse," 11, 132
Eczema, 46
Egg and spoon race, 153, 159
Elbow, capped, 44
Encephalomyelitis, 49
Endurance, horse's, 5–7
English fox hound, 97
"English" saddle, 100, 146
Equitation, 69–77
  bibliography, 202
Escort, mounted, 191–192
Etiquette, beagling and bassetting, 114
  fox hunting, 101–102
European hare, 109–110
Ewe neck, 32
Exhaustion, treatment for, 41
Exmoor ponies, 9
Extended gallop, 8, 186
"Exterminator," 132
Eye ailments, 49

Fables, horses and, 21–26
Facón, 175
Famous horses of famous men, 17
Farcy, 48
Farrier, 56
Fault and out, 88
Feather, 49
Feather-edged shoe, 55
Feathers, 96
Federation Equestre Internationale (F.E.I.),
  85
  types of competition under rules of, 88
Fences, 168–169
Fender, 169

Field, beagling and bassetting, 113
  fox hunting, 101
Field master, beagling or bassetting, 113
  fox hunting, 95, 100, 101
Filly, 5
Finish pole, 131
Firing, 51
First aid, 41
First Troop Philadelphia City Cavalry, 186
First use of horses, 17
Fistules, 46
Fistulous withers, 46
Fitzwilliam girth, 62, 63, 100
Flag race, 161–162
Flank cinch, 172
Flaps, saddle, 61, 100
Flask, 100
Flat racing, 127–133
  barometer of, 133
  bibliography, 203
  classic races, 128
  direction horses run in, 129
  distances, 129
  establishments, 127–128
  governing bodies, 132
  history, 127
  records, 129
  terms, 129–131
  produce, 129
  tracks, 127
Flexion, 74
"Flora Temple," 138
"Flying Dutchman," 129
Foaled (term defined), 5
Foals, 5
  diseases of, 50
Foaled leather girth, 61, 62, 100
Forage, 35
  uneaten, as sign of sickness, 41
Forehand, turn to the right on the, 70
Forelegs, joints of, 30
  lameness in, 42
Forging, 32, 50
Forward seat, 69
Founder, 43
Fox, 95–97
  gray, 96
  nicknames, 95
  red, 95, 96
  straight necked, 96
Fox Catcher Farm, 121
Fox hounds, 97–98
  American, 97
  attributes of, 97–98
  bay of, 98
  blooding, 98
  casting, 95
  crossbreed, 97
  drag, 98
  ear markings, 98
  English, 97
  roading, 98
  walking, 98
  young entry, 98
Fox hunting, 95–105
  bibliography, 203
  dress, 102–105
  etiquette, 101–102
  governing body, 105
  lore, 105
  organized hunts, 105
  positions of hunt staff, 95
  tack, 99–100
Fox Stake, 141
Fox trot, 8, 74, 86
Free for all race, 139

French coach horse, 10
Fresh-legged, 141
Frog, of horse's hoof, 30
Funeral horse, 24
Furlong, 129
Futurity, the, 128

Gag, 64, 65
Gaits, 8, 73–74, 86
   faulty, 31–32
"Gallant Fox," 131
"Gallant Man," 131
Gallop, 8, 73
   collected, 186
   extended, 8, 186
Galvayne's groove, 30
Games, gaucho, 176–177
Garden State Handicap, 128
Garden State Stakes, 128
Garrison finish, 130
Gauchos, see Cowboys
Gelding, 5
"George Wilkes," 138
German coach horse, 10
Gestation period, 5, 50
Get up a hare (term explained), 110
Girths, 61–63
   types of, 61–63, 100
   used in fox hunting, 100
   Western, 169
Glanders, 48, 51
Godolphin Barb, 11, 133
God's, mythological, associated with horses, 25
"Golden Miller," 122
Gone to ground (term explained), 96
Grain, 35, 36
"Grand Circuit," 139–140
Grand National Steeplechase, 122–123
"Great Heart," 8
Green horses, 86
Green Mountain (Vermont) Horse Association, 3
Gretna green race, 153
"Greyhound," 138, 141
Grooming, 35, 36, 37, 41
   equipment, 36, 37
   resisting, 50
Ground tie, 165, 168
Guest judges, 83
Gymkhana, 153–162

Hackamore bridle, 64
Hackles, 98
Hackney (English trotting horse), 10, 81
Hackney ponies, 11
Hall, riding, 76
Halter, 64, 65
Halter pulling, 37, 50
"Hambletonian," 137, 138
Hambletonian Stake, 141
Hammers, 56
Handicap, 129
Hands, good, meaning of, 69
   term used in measuring height), 4
Hares, 109–111
   enemies of, 110
   European, 109–110
   referred to as she, 110
Harness horses, see Pacers; Trotters
Harness racing, 137–142
   bibliography, 204
   fixtures, 141
   "Grand Circuit," 139–140
   records, 141–142
   terms, 140–141
   track, 140

Hat, Stetson, 170
Haunches, turn to the right on the, 70
Hay, 35, 36, 41
Hazer, 173
Head ailments, 48
Headpiece, 63
Health, good, maintenance of, 41
"Heatherbloom," 8
Heaves, 49
Hedge, as obstacle, 120
Heels, contracted, 43, 55
Height, horse's, 4
   cavalry mounts, 184
   hunters, 98
"Henry Clay," 138
Hereford cattle, 165
"Herod," 11
Herring gut, 32
Hide ailments, 46–47
Hide bound, 46
High blowing, 49
High jump, 8
Hindlegs, joints of, 30
   lameness in, 42
Hinny, 14
Hippodrome, built for horse events at Olympian Games, 17
Hippogriff, 24
Historical data, concerning horses, 17–18
Hobble, 170
Hobby Horse, 22
Hock, capped, 44
Hog back obstacle, 86
Hogged (term explained), 4
Holding up cubs, 95
Holy Cross Day, 25
Honda, 172
Honor show, 81
Hoof, 30, 37
   ailments, 42–4
   cracked, 43, 55
Hoof pick, 36
Hopeful Stakes, 128
Hopples, 138, 141
Horn, fox hunting, 100
   used in beagling and bassetting, 113
Horse, see Stallion
Horse encephalitis, 49
Horse shows, 81–91
   bibliography, 202
   catalog, 87
   classes, types of, 85
   classification of, 81–82
   classification of individuals, 84–85
   governing body, 81
   guide for managers, officers and committees, 90–91
   high score awards, 90
   hunters, 87
   important, 88
   judges, 83
   judge's score card, 89
   jumpers, 85
   Maclay, The, 90
   officials, 82, 90–91
   protests, 90
   ribbons, 83–84
   scurry, 87
   stake, 87
   stewards, 82–83
   Western Division, 174
Horseman Stake, 141
Horsemanship, test of, 194–197
Horshoes, see also Plates; Shoeing; Shoes
   in mythology, 21
   types, 55

211

Hounds, see also Bassetts; Beagles; Fox hounds
  coupled, 97, 111
Houyhnhnms, The, 25
Huaso, 175
Hunt race meeting, 119, 120
Hunt races, 119, 120
Hunt, staff, beagling and bassetting, 113
  fox hunting, 95, 100–101
Hunters, 4, 10, 81, 87
  classification of, 87
  conformation, 87
  corinthian class, 87
  fox hunting, 98–99
  good, characteristics of, 98–99
  green, 86
  horse shows, 87
  obstacles, 87
  qualified, 87
  working class, 87
Hunting cap, 102, 103
Hunting coat, 102
Hunting saddle, 61
Hunting seat, 69, 70, 90
Huntsman, beagling and bassetting, 113
  fox hunting, 95, 100
  Honorary, 100, 113
Hurdle race, 119–120
Hurdles, 119, 120
Hussars, 182, 183

Iceland pony, 9
Illustrators, famous for horses, 18
In and out obstacle, 86, 87
"Incitatus," 25
Indirect rein, 70, 71
Individual Dressage Competition (Olympic Games), 88
Infectious anemia, 48–49
Influenza, 48
Insignia, Cavalry's, 181
Interfering, see Brushing
Irons, see Stirrups

"Jack Horner," 122
Jackrabbit, blacktail, 109–110
Jacks (male hares), 110
Jacks, see Asses
Jeans, cowboy's, 171
Jennet, 14
Jockey Club, 87, 131, 132
Jockeys, famous, 132
Jog, 74
Joints, horse's, 30
Judges, horse show, 83
  score card, 89
Jughead, 141
Jump, broad, 8
  high, 8
Jumpers, 85–86
  green, 86
  judge's score card, 89
  obstacles for, 85–86
  scoring, 85
Jumping, 74
"Justin Morgan," 138

"Kellsboro Jack," 122
Kent Mare, The, 138
Kentucky Derby, 128
Kiang wild ass, 9
Kicking, 37, 50
"Kincsem," 132
Kladruber horse, 12
Kulan wild ass, 9
"Kings Own," 8

"Lady Suffolk," 138

Lameness, 41–42
  evidence of, 42
  mixed, 42
  swinging, 42
  supporting-leg, 41
Laminitis, 43
Lampas, 48
Lancers, 182, 183
Lariats, 171–172
Laryngitis, 48
Lasso, 171, 175
Latigo, 169
Lead, left, 72
  right, 72
Leading rein, 70, 71
Led pony race, 156–157
Left lead, 72
Leg bandages, 65
Legends, about horses, 21–26
Legs, ailments, 44–46
  joints of, 30
  swollen (big), 45
Leverets, 110
Levis, 171
Liberty horses, 13
Lice, 46–47
Ligaments, 30
Light horses, 9–11
Limit class, 85
Linseed, 35
Lip strap, 63, 65
Lipizzan horse, 12
Little Brown Jug, 141
Liverpool obstacle, 86, 122, 123
Livestock record associations, 200–201
Llanero, 175
Longden, J., 132
Longeing, 74, 75
Longhorn cattle, 166
Lonsdale girth, 62, 63, 100
Lope, 74
"Lou Dillon," 138, 142
Lung ailments, 47

Maclay, The, 90
Maiden, 130
Maiden class, 85
"Major," 25
'Malarial' fever, 48
Mallein injection, 51
Mallet, polo, 145, 146
"Mambrino Chief," 137, 138
"Man o' War," 132
Management, stable, 35–38
  bibliography, 201
Mane, hogged, 4
  itchy, 46
Mane and tail comb, 36
Mange, 47
Marches, Cavalry, 185–186
Mare, 5, 13
"Marengo," 17
"Mare's nest," 23
Markings, horse's, 3
Martingales, 99, 146
Mash, bran, 35, 41
Maryland Hunt Cup, 121
Mask, 96, 110
Master carries the horn (term explained), 101
"Master Crump," 8
Master of Bassetts, 113
Master of Beagles, 113
Master of Fox Hounds (MFH), 95, 100
Masters of Foxhounds Association of America, 105
"Matchem," 11

Maverick, 168
McClellan saddle, 185, 190
Measurement of height, 4
Medical supplies, basic, 50–51
Megrims, 49
Merthiolate, 41, 51
"Messenger," 137, 138
Messenger Stake, 141
Metaphen, 41, 51
Middle distance, 130
Military saddle, 61
Milk teeth, 29
Millet, 35
Monmouth Handicap, 128
Moon blindness, 49
"Mopsus," 129
Morgan horse, 10, 11, 12, 81, 184
'Mountain' fever, 48
Mounted drill, 193–194
Mounted escort, 191–192
Mounted police, 189–190
Mounted wrestling, 162
Mud fever, 44
Mules, 13–14, 184
Murphy, Isaac, 132
Muscles, ailments, 46–47
Musical chairs, 153
Musical hats, 155
Mustang, 10–11
Myths, horses and, 21–26

Nail, shoe, 55
"Nancy Hanks," 138, 141
National Beagle Club, 109
Navicular disease, 43
Near horses, 13–14
Near side, 8
Neck ailments, 48
Neckerchief, cowboy's, 170
"Nelson," 17
New Forest ponies, 9
Nightmares, 23
"Nigra," 8
North America, first horses in, 17
Norwegian dun, 9
Nose band, 63, 64, 99
Novice class, 85
Number of horses in U.S., 13

Oats, 35–36
Objection, 131
Obstacles, for hunters, 87
    for jumpers, 85–86
    steeplechasing, 120, 121
Odds-on, 130
Off side, 8
Officers' Field Saddle, 185
Officials, show, 82
"Old Bill," 4
"Old Bones," 132
"Old Whitey," 17
Olympic Games, equestrian events at, 17,
    88
"Omaha," 131
Onager wild ass, 9
Ophthalmia, 49
Organizations, horse, 197–201
Origin, of horse, 17
Orloff breed, 11
Out on the limb (term explained), 141
Outlaw, 168
"Overall," 8
Overgirth, 63, 65
Overreaching, 32, 50
Oxer obstacle, 86

Pace, 8, 73, 138
    stepping, 74, 86

Pacers, 137
Pad, 96, 110
Padding (faulty gait), 31
Paddock polo, 150
Paint, see Piebald
Painters, famous for horses, 18, 174–175
Paintings, old, of horses, 17–18
"Pale Horse of the Saxons," 22
Palomino, 3, 12, 81
Panel, 101
Pari-mutuel, 130
Park gait, 86
Parlay, 130
Pasterns, 31
Pathological shoeing, 55–56
Pato, el, 176
Patron deities, 25
Patron Saint of horsemen, 25
Pegasus, 24
Pelham, 64, 65, 99, 146
Percheron draft horse, 11
"Peter the Great," 138
"Phar Lap," 132
Phillips Training Saddle, 185
Photo-finish, 131
Pick up man, 173
Piebald, 3, 168
"Pilot Jr.," 138
Pincers, 56, 57
Pinfiring, 51
Pink (term explained), 102
Pinto, see Piebald
Plater, 131
Plates, 131
Place, 130
Plank fence obstacle, 87
Pleurisy, 47
Pneumonia, 47
Point-to-point (race), 119
Pole, 131, 141
Police mounts, 189–190
Poll evil, 47
Polo, 145–150
    bibliography, 204
    clothing, 146
    governing body, 150
    handicaps, 147–148
    history, 148–149
    indoor, 145
    outdoor, 145
    periods ("chukkers"), 146
    Round Robin, 149–150
    rules, 147
    tack, 146
Polo ball stroking contest, 153
Polo mounts, height, 4, 146
    weight, 4, 146
Polo saddle, 61
Pommel, 61
Ponies, breeds, 9, 11–12
    Chincoteague, 12
    Connemara, 9
    Cumberland, 9
    Dartmouth, 9
    Exmoor, 9
    Hackney, 11
    height of, 4
    Iceland (Celtic), 9
    New Forest, 9
    polo, see Polo mounts
    Shetland, 9, 11, 81
    weight, 4
    Welsh, 11, 81
    Westmoreland, 9
Pony Express, 174
Port, 64, 65

Post and rail obstacle, 86, 87, 120
Potato picking scramble, 157–158
Preakness, The, 128
Preston brand, 184
"Prince Friarstown," 149
Prints, old, of horses, 17–18
Pritchel, 56, 57
Prix des Nations (Olympic Games), 88
Prize list, 87
Produce race, 130
Professional, 84
Professional Horsemen's Association of America (P.H.A.), 88, 90, 198
Prophetic horses, 23
Protests, at horse shows, 90
Przewalski's horse, see Tarpan
Puissance, 88
Pulling leather, 75
Pulse, abnormal, as sign of sickness, 41
    normal rate, 41
Purebred, use of term, 11
Puss (nickname for hares), 110

Quagga, 9
Quarter boots, 138
Quarter clips, 55
Quarter horses, 10, 11, 165
    number of, 13
Quinella, 130
Quirt, 170
Quittor, 43

Rabbits, see also Hares; Jackrabbit cottontail, 110–111
Races, allowance, 129
    balloon, 158–159
    bar, 139
    bareback, 154
    claiming, 129–130
    classic (flat racing), 128
    classified, 139
    egg and spoon, 153, 159
    flag, 161–162
    free for all, 139
    Gretna green, 153
    hunt, 119, 120
    hurdle, 119–120
    important (harness racing), 141
    led pony, 156–157
    produce, 130
    relay, 154
    saddle relay, 158
    saddling and bridling, 153–154
    sharpshooters, 160–161
    shirt, 157
    team relay bending, 154–155
    vegetable, 160
    water, 153
Racing, see Flat racing; Harness racing; steeplechasing
Racing colors, 131, 132
Racing saddle, 61
Racing seat, 127
Rack, 8, 73, 86
Ranches, cattle, 166
    horse, 165
Range cattle, 165–166
Range horses, 165
Rasp, 56, 57
Ratcatcher, 102
Rating, 130
Rearing, 50
Registered horse, 86
Registered judges, 83
"Regret," 128
Rein, bearing, 70, 71
    direct, 70, 71

indirect, 70, 71
    leading, 70, 71
Reins, 63, 64–65
    fox hunting, 99
    using two sets of, 75
Relay race, 154
Remount, 184, 189
Remount stations, 184
Removing the saddle contest, 154
Remuda, 168, 176
Riata, 171
Ribbons, horse-show, 83–84
    on hunting cap, 103
Ribs, horse's, 29
Richards, Sir Gordon, 132
Riders, steeplechase, 121
Riding, cross-country, 6–7, 8
Riding hall, 76
Riding herd, 168
Riding horses, height, 4
    pasterns, 31
    shoulders, 31
    weight, 4
"Rienzi" (Winchester), 17
Right lead, 72
Ringbone, 44–45
Ringer, 131
Ringworm, 47
Roached, see Hogged
Roading hounds, 98
Roan, 3
Roaring, 49
Rodeo Association of America, 173
Rodeos, 172–173
Roller, 65
Romal, 170
Roman nose, 32
Round Robin (polo match), 149–150
Roundup, 168
"Roustabout," 8
Rub rag, 36
"Rubio," 122
Running through foil (term explained), 110
Running walk, 8, 73, 86
Ruptured tendon, 45
Rustler, 168
"Ruthless," 128

Sacred Nails, The, 25
Sacrifice, horses offered as, 25
Saddle cloths, 65
Saddle horse saddle, 61
Saddle horse seat, 69, 90
Saddle horses, 86
    American, 10, 11
Saddle relay race, 158
Saddles, 61
    "English," 100, 146
    fox hunting, 100
    McClellan, 185, 190
    Officers' Field, 185
    Phillips Training, 185
    Saumur, 185
    stock (Western), 61, 169, 175
    types, 61
    weight of, 61
    Whitman, 190
Saddlesore, 47
Saddling, resisting, 50
Saddling and bridling race, 153–154
Sagittarius, 44
"Sailor's Horse," 22–23
Salt, 35
Salto de la maroma, el, 176–177
"Salvator," 129
Sand crack, 43
Sande, Earl, 132

Sandshifter, 140
Sandwich case, 100
Santa Anita Handicap, 128
Santa Gertrudis cattle, 166
Sapling Stakes, 128
Saumur saddle, 185
Scarlet hunting coat, 102
Scent, breast high, 96
Schools, foreign cavalry, 186
Score card, judge's (horse shows), 89
Scoring (harness racing term), 140
Scraper, 36
Sculptors, famous for horses, 18
Scurry, 87
Scut, 110
Sea horses, 23
Seat, dressage, 69
　faults, 70
　forward, 69
　good, meaning of, 69
　hunting, 69, 70, 90
　racing, 127
　saddle horse, 69, 90
　steeplechase, 123
　stock (Western), 69, 70, 90, 170
"Sergeant Murphy," 122
Sesamoiditis, 45
Set of couples, 100
Shank, 64
Sharpshooters race, 160–161
Sheep, 167
Shetland ponies, 9, 11, 81
Shire draft horse, 11
Shirt race, 157
Shoe boil, 44, 46
Shoeing, 55–57
　bibliography, 201
　cold, 56
　correct normal, 56
　need for, 55
　pathological, 55–56
　poor, 56
　steps in, 56
Shoemaker, Willie, 132
Shoes, see also Plates
　changing, 56
　nails, 55
　polo ponies', 147
　types of, 55
　weighted, 138
Shorthorn cattle, 166
Shotgun chaps, 171
Shoulders, 31
　lameness in, 42
Show, 130
Shows, see Horse shows
Shying, 50
Sickness, indications of, 41
Side saddle, 61
Sidebone, 43
Sidewheeler, 140
Single foot (gait), 8, 74
"Sir Barton," 131
Sire, 5
Sitfast, 46, 47
Skewbald, 3, 168
Skirts, saddle, 61
Sleeping sickness, 49
'Slow' fever, 48
Slow gait, 8, 74, 86
Slow trot, 75
Snaffle, 64, 65
Snaffle bit, 63, 99
Snaffle reins, 63, 64–65, 75
Snake fence obstacle, 87
Snip (marking), 3

Sole, 30
　bruised, 42
Soreback, 37–38, 47
Sores, open, first aid for, 41
Sorrel, 3
Spavings, 45
Splay foot, 31
Splint, 45
Sponge, 36
Sprain, 45
Sprint, 130
Spurs, 103, 171
Squadron A (Cavalry guard organization), 186
Squadron of Cavalry, 5
Squat, 110
Stable (racing) colors, 65, 131, 132
Stable management, 35–38
　bibliography, 201
Stable vices, 37, 49–50
Staggers, 49
Stake, in horse shows, 87
Stakes, 129
Stallions, 5, 14
　breeding and, 50
　dimensions of, 38
Stalls, dimensions of, 38
Standardbreds, 10, 11, 137, 138, 184
　American, 137
　classification, 139
　famous mares, 138
　famous sires, 137, 138
　number of, 13
Standards, Cavalry's, 181
Standing (straight) stall, dimensions of, 38
Star (marking), 3
"Star Pointer," 142
Stayer distance, 130
Steep hill, riding down a, 74
Steeplechase, defined, 119
Steeplechase seat, 123
Steeplechasing, 119–124
　courses, 120, 121
　bibliography, 203–204
　definitions, 123
　history, 123
　minimum weight permitted, 121
　obstacles, 120
　riders, 121
　rules, 123–124
Steer, 166
Stepping pace, 74, 86
Sterns, 112
Stetson hat, 170
Stewards, A.H.S.A., 82–83
Stifled, 45
Stirrup leather, 101
Stirrups, 62, 63
　fox hunting, 100
Stock horses, 174
Stock (Western) saddle, 61, 169, 175
Stock (Western) seat, 69, 70, 90, 170
Stomach, horse's, 30
　ailments, 47
Stone wall obstacle, 88
Stopping the earth (term defined), 96
Straight necked fox, 96
Straight stall, dimensions of, 38
Strains, 45
Strangles, 48
Stride, horse's, 8, 138
Striking with forefeet, 50
String girth, 62, 63
Stringhalt, 45
Stumbling, 75
Suburban Handicap, 128
Suffolk draft horse, 11

Suicide horse, 25
Sulky, 137
Sunfishing, 173
Superstition, horses and, 21–22, 65
Surcingle, 65
'Swamp' fever, 48
"Swaps," 129
Sweeney, 47
Sweepstakes, 129
Swimming, 75
Swollen leg, 45
"Sword Dancer," 132
Symbols, horses and, 21

Tack, 61–65
  bibliography, 202
  Cavalry, 185
  fox hunting, 99–100
  mounted police, 190
  polo, 146
  western, 169–170
Tacking a horse, order of precedence in, 65
Tail, docked, 4
  itchy, 46
Tail rubbing, 37, 50
Take to covert (term explained), 110
Tang horses of Chinese art, 18
"Tanya," 128
Tapadero, 169, 170
Tarpan (Przewalski's horse), 9
Team relay bending race, 154–155
Teeth, horse's, 29–30
Temple Gwathmey (steeplechase), 123
Tendons, 30
  bowed, 44
  ruptured, 45
Tennessee walking horse, 10, 11, 81
Tetanus, 47
Tetanus antitoxin, 51
Thoroughbred Racing Association, 132
Thoroughbreds, 10, 11, 121, 132, 146, 165,
  184, 189
  foundation sires of the, 11
  names, 131
  number of, 13
Thoroughpin, 46
Three quarter shoe, 55
Throat latch, 63
Thrush, 37, 43–44
Tied in (conformation fault), 31
Timber obstacles, 120, 121
"Titan Hanover," 138
Toe-weights, 141
Tongs, 56
Tools, blacksmith's, 56, 57
  grooming, 36, 37
"Totalisator," 130
"Tote," 130
"Touraine," 8
"Track please," meaning of term, 76
Tracks, flat racing, 127
  harness racing, 140
"Traveler," 17
Travers, the, 128
Tree, saddle, 61, 175
Triple bar obstacle, 86
"Triple Crown" events, 128
"Triple Crown Winners," 128, 131–132
Trojan Horse, 22
Tropilla, 176
Trot, 8, 73, 86, 138, 186
  fox, 8
  slow, 75
  time required to cover a mile, 6, 7
Trotters, 137
Trotting horse, American, 10, 11
Trotting register, 139

Tushes, 29
"Twenty Grand," 132
Twice around, 141
Twitch, 37
Two-tracking, 71

Unicorn, 24
United Hunts Racing Association, 123,
  199–200
United States Equestrian Team (U.S.E.T.),
  88, 90, 199
United States Polo Association, 148, 150
United States Pony Clubs, Inc., 197–198
United States Trotting Association, 139
Up on the bit, 72
Up-wind, 97

Vaquero, 168, 175
Vegetable race, 160
Veterinarian, when to call for services of,
  41, 47, 50, 51–52
Vices, stable, 37, 49–50
Vise, 56
Vitamin-mineral supplements, 35
Vixen (female fox), 95

Walk, 8, 73, 86, 186
  running, 8, 73, 86
  time required to cover a mile, 6, 7
Walking horse, Tennessee, 10, 11, 81
Walking hounds, 98
Walk-over, 123
Wall, of horse's hoof, 30
"War Admiral," 5, 132
Water, drinking, 8, 36
Water race, 153
Weaning, 5
Weaving, 37, 50
Weight, horse's, 4
  at foaling, 5
  cavalry mounts, 184
  hunters, 98
Westchester ("National") Cup, 149
Western Harness Racing Association, 141
Western saddle, 61, 169, 175
Western seat, 69, 70, 90, 170
Whippers-in, beagling and bassetting, 113
  fox hunting, 95, 100
  Honorary, 113
Whips, foxhunting, 101
  used in beagling and bassetting, 113
"Whirlaway," 132
Whistling, 49
White gate obstacle, 87
White horses, 21, 22, 25
Whitman saddle, 190
Wiggler, 140
Wild asses, 9
Wild horses, 9
Wind ailments, 49
Windgall, 46
Windpuff, 46
Wind-sucking, 37, 50
Wire cutters, carried by huntsmen, 100
Withers, fistulous, 46
Withers, The, 128
Wolf teeth, 29
Worms, 46, 47
Wounds, minor, first aid for, 41
Wrangler, 168
Wrestling, mounted, 162

"Xanthus," 23

Zebras, 8, 9, 14
  Burchell's, 9
  Grevy's, 9
  Mountain, 9
Zebrass, 14